C000215768

THE GREAT
BORDERS FLOOD
of 1948

THE GREAT
BORDERS FLOOD
of 1948

LAWSON WOOD

TEMPUS

First published 2002

PUBLISHED IN THE UNITED KINGDOM BY:
Tempus Publishing Ltd
The Mill, Brimscombe Port
Stroud, Gloucestershire GL5 2QG
www.tempus-publishing.com

PUBLISHED IN THE UNITED STATES OF AMERICA BY:
Tempus Publishing Inc.
2 Cumberland Street
Charleston, SC 29401
USA
www.tempuspublishing.com

British Library Cataloguing in Publication Data.
A catalogue record for this book is available from the British Library.

ISBN 0 7524 2756 3

Typesetting and origination by Tempus Publishing.
PRINTED AND BOUND IN GREAT BRITAIN.

Acknowledgements

Margaret Squires for her extensive collection of 'official' photographs; Linda Bankier, Borough Archivist for Berwick upon Tweed Borough Council; Tweeddale Press Group; *Haddington Courier*; Fantasy Prints; Lesley Orson; Lindsay Wood; Alastair Scott for his insight and knowledge on the plight of the local railways; Mark Fairbairn; James Borthwick Manuel; Bill Cormack; Barbara Wood; Richard Taylor & Ed Bartholomew at the National Railway Museum, York; Wendy Reid from the Eyemouth, East Berwickshire Partnership; Selkirk Library Archives; Sheila Northcott and Veronica Wallace from The History Unit of the Haddington Library Service; Richard Hunter, Edinburgh City Archivist, Edinburgh City Council; The Eyemouth Museum; Scottish Records Office; The Scottish Executive; Ian Allen Ltd; The Royal Bank of Scotland; Bank of Scotland; Barclays' Bank; *The Railway Magazine*; *The Railway Gazette*; *Railway World*; *Directory of Railway Officials Yearbook*; *Scottish Geographical Magazine*; Meteorological Office, Scotland; The *Gresley Observer*; Minutes of the Railway Executive, August 1948; National Farmers' Union.

August 1948

Surprisingly, the Borders are actually renowned as being one of two locations having the least rainfall in the entire United Kingdom (the other being East Anglia). But when it does rain! Well – watch out, as it may all happen at the same time! The Scottish Borders hadn't seen sustained rainfall like this for over 100 years and various newspapers commented on this. In fact much of Europe was also similarly hit; there were heavy snowfalls in Switzerland, ninety-mile-an-hour gales in Belgium and over 36 million tons of rain fell in Berlin over two days. Vital crops were lost and holidaymakers' and hoteliers' plans were wrecked. 1948 appears to have been particularly bad for many other parts of the world too. Even New York had its heaviest snowfall ever recorded (which still hasn't been beaten yet). Not much consolation for those in the midst of it, here in the Borders.

A new lake formed on Prenderguest Farm west of Ayton when a major culvert collapsed and flood waters collected in the low-lying farmland. (Margaret Squires Collection)

A view of the new lake looking east towards the embankment. The now crumbling embankment held at bay some 4 million tons of flood water, threatening all the low-lying area of Eyemouth harbour. (National Railway Museum, York. Collection: NRM 07/02 Number: 126/11/64)

They said it could never happen again after the winter floods the year before. 11 January in fact had seen widespread flooding due to snow-melt and heavy rainfall, with a number of roads blocked, but here they were again, in midsummer, this time after a continuous deluge over a twenty-four-hour period. The River Tweed was able to cope with much of the runoff in its wide basin, and had the room to expand to twice its normal size, but smaller rivers such as the Tyne at Haddington, the Biel, the Blackadder, Whiteadder Water, River Till and the River Eye were disasters waiting to happen. Part of the Tweed basin that August would receive more than a third of its annual rainfall in only six days!

The problem wasn't just the strength of the deluge over the twenty-four hours which created the flood, it was the amount of rain which had fallen during the previous two weeks. In August the *'Glorious 12th'* was undoubtedly exceptional; over four inches of rain had fallen the previous week and at least another four inches the week before that.

There had also been no sun or wind in the entire two weeks prior to the flood; the rivers were already at bursting point and had been for some time, the waterlogged land just couldn't soak up any more rain water and it was only a matter of time before the likelihood of a flood became a reality.

The River Eye had flooded in the past and would do so again, this time in a very short space of time. Unnatural barriers, such as railway lines, had forever changed the geography and topography of the countryside and whilst conduits, culverts and spillways were constructed, there was no guessing just how much water they had to contend with. This was made painfully obvious when a major overspill culvert, over three yards in diameter, collapsed at a railway embankment west of Eyemouth and rainwater and debris collected in the low lying farm land.

The railway line between Reston & Cockburnspath was also severely hit when the River Eye burst its banks, with almost every bridge washed away. Cumledge Mill near Duns was virtually destroyed by a wall of water and whilst there were very real problems all along the Tweed Valley basin and East Lothian, the impending doom of the small fishing town of Eyemouth tended to take precedence over many more heart-rending stories of loss and tragedy at the height of the flood. That and the total shut-down of all cross-border rail travel gripped the nation's attention for weeks.

This is a brief account of the rain-sodden weeks of August 1948 and the aftermath of the flood in the lives of those more unfortunate than us in the Borders and East Lothian, and how six inches of rain would affect some of their lives forever.

James Buchan was quoted in a BBC newscast in 1948 on the flood devastation 'Rain did in a few hours what Hitler and his bombers couldn't do in six years. It closed the Scottish end of the great East Coast route from Edinburgh to London.'

Cumledge Mill and the workers' homes near Duns would suffer severe damage when flood waters inundated them to a depth of over seven feet, destroying machinery, vehicles and a number of homes. (Lawson Wood Collection)

Sunday 8 August

A bit early in the season for rain some said, but at this stage the heavy rainfall was still seen as no real threat to the harvest or to the holiday season. Not exactly the best of summers, but Margaret Tait was still crowned the Eyemouth Herring Queen in mid-July and the colourful pageant of fishing boats and town processions were once more extremely popular with locals and tourists alike. The sea was kind that day with the local fishing fleet all out bedecked with bunting and full to bursting with passengers, led by the Herring Queen and her maids from St Abbs to Eyemouth harbours on the high tide.

However, August was another matter – dark clouds, high winds, rough seas and rain did little to improve the holiday makers' spirits. Local farmers were in some distress as to whether they would be able to harvest their crops as much had already been flattened by the rain. All of the rivers were running brown as soil continued to wash off the land and end up far out to sea.

The River Eye, some 14½ miles long, rises near Grantshouse in an area the locals call the 'Moon' – children love telling of how the River Eye is the longest river in the world as it starts at the Moon! What was once a rivulet as it travelled alongside its two companions, the East Coast Main Line railway and the A1 trunk road, was now a raging torrent. With no let up, rain continued to pound the countryside. The staff at Grantshouse railway station were now casting concerned looks at the River Eye nearby as it gathered in speed and volume and battered against the embankment

THE HARBOUR, EYEMOUTH.   J.15168

Who would have thought the peaceful fishing harbour of Eyemouth would be the scene of such destruction in a very short span of time. (Lawson Wood Collection)

Smaller boats and cobbles moored nearby the sluice gates were the first to receive the force of the flood waters, when the spate poured over the pier into the small craft, sinking them. (Margaret Squires Collection)

which held the main line railway. The force of the River Tweed also gathered momentum as all of her tributaries flooded. Rain water continued to pound the Borders countryside, with the highest amounts being recorded around the Kelso area.

Even at low tide at 11 a.m., the river was in full flood and the high pier at the entrance to Eyemouth Harbour was covered by the spate. Rising flood waters in Eyemouth, coupled with an onshore gale, produced even higher tides that same day and the river poured over the sluice gates and three boats which lay broadside to the flood were sunk. The *Catherine* and the *Maplin* were lost but the *Naid* was later recovered.

Weatherhead's boat-building yard was by this time also awash and the houses at Bridgend at the bottom of the Bane Mill Brae had to be evacuated by mid-afternoon. 'The rain just didn't want to stop,' said some Eyemouth residents as they tried to negotiate a path back up the brae avoiding the thousands of pieces of firewood, logs and debris which continued to pile up at the edge of the flood water level.

Eyemouth beach by this time was totally unrecognisable as the debris from the river was spread everywhere. The sea was tinged a dull muddy orange colour which extended over a mile out from the river mouth at the entrance of Eyemouth Harbour. At the mouth of the River Tweed, the brown waters of the spate spread over five miles out to sea and her protective sand bar was covered in log debris. The rough seas and onshore wind meant that these log piles were unable to be dispersed. Local residents took advantage of this windfall, by stocking up on logs for fuel for the

The low-lying area of Eyemouth was quickly overcome by the force of the water not only coming down the river, but also from the approach roads, particularly the steep road at Northburn (the author's former home). Well named, this ancient burn turned into 'north river'. (Barbara Wood)

Opposite: My mother and father's house at Northburn (seen here) was quickly inundated by the flood waters. Hastily produced sand bags failed to stop the water's ingress. A temporary wall of Calor Gas bottles was placed by my father, Rob, to try and divert the worst of the flow of water away from the front door, but this proved ineffective and the gas bottles were washed down the High Street. (Barbara Wood)

winter months. Thankfully by around 6.30 that evening, the rain had lessened inland and the spate had subsided enough to let the residents move back into the cottages in Eyemouth and start to clean up the devastation in their homes. This was just a small reprieve as more rain was still to follow.

Over the following few days the rain continued to pound the Tweed and Eye Valleys, river levels were at an all-time dangerous high and it was only a matter of time before they burst their banks and invaded so many people's homes and businesses.

6.30 p.m. Wednesday 11 August

It's still raining! A shallow depression had made its way slowly eastwards into the North Sea; there it met an almost stationary warm front to the north of this system. This brought heavy rains, firstly into the Yorkshire and Durham areas, but its focus was going to be Berwickshire and East Lothian. The high ground of the Lammermuirs and Cheviots was already sodden, most rivers and tributaries were already near bursting point. Minor landslips had already occurred on some of the higher ground, it was only a matter of time before flooding would occur, but no one could guess at the devastating effect it would have in such a short space of time.

	Tweed	Bruton *square miles*	Norwich
more than 6 in.	8	85	268
more than 5 in.	130	288	720
more than 4 in.	800	809	1,071
more than 3 in.	1,525	1,931	2,007
more than 2 in.	2,900	4,419	3,827

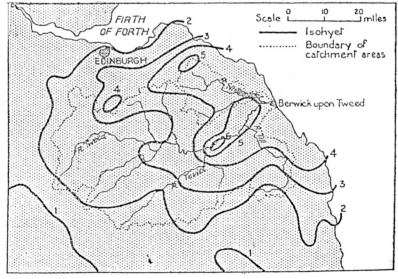

Rainfall map of 12 August 1948. (Meteorological Office, Edinburgh)

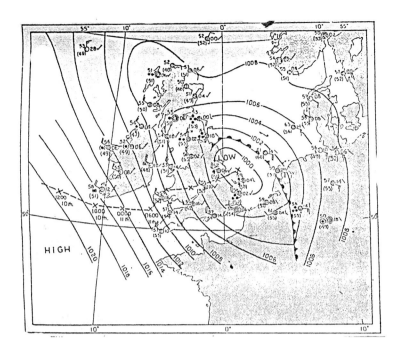

Synoptic chart, 06.00 GMT 12 August 1948. (Meteorological Office, Edinburgh)

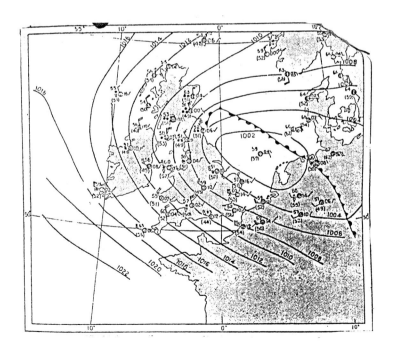

15

4 a.m. Thursday 12 August

The meteorological office forecast local showers! However, some forecasters warned that the rain coming from the south east could have devastating consequences on the Borders and East Lothian countryside. Rainfall was by now torrential and had no indication of letting up. The rivers were once more rising rapidly and small landslides were being created wherever the excess water run off the surrounding farmland into the rivers. At the end of the day over 400 million tons of water would fall on the Tweed & Eye Valley systems.

The River Till was the first to burst its banks and breach the old embankment first placed by the Culley family at Akeld in the early nineteenth century; the top of its twisting line was the only visible ground. At the confluence of the Glen, the River Till spread over some 6,000 acres of arable land to a depth of several feet.

This new lake extended up the Glen Valley to Kirknewton. This, combined with the College Burn at West Newton, cut through its right bank and took a more direct route through Kirknewton flooding a large number of houses and the local Post Office. Sand, mud and gravel deposits covered otherwise good arable land. All road and rail services from Kirknewton up the Bowmont Valley were severed. The

The River Till to the south of the Tweed soon burst its banks and spread over 6,000 acres of arable and pasture land. (Margaret Squires Collection)

Railway bridges were swept away by the force and speed of the rising flood waters, leaving railway lines exposed and severing all water and electric services to many communities.

Millfield road was torn up and the bridge from West Newton to Crookhouse collapsed. Up above Wooler in Happy Valley, one road bridge completely disappeared under the level of the water. When the river took a new route at Earle Mill it left its bridge high and dry! Over the next six years, £110,000 would have to be spent on the River Till Improvement Scheme.

The old Iron Bridge in Wooler listed badly and finally collapsed, cutting all power, gas and water supplies to Weetwood Avenue. An old War Department hut just below the bridge was evacuated just minutes before its foundations were swept away and destroyed. Over 3ft of water covered the bowling green and it spread over Station Road to a depth of just over 2ft.

The River Beamish burst its banks at Brandon and flooded Powburn Village for the third time in just three years and a steel bridge on the Wooler to Chatton Road shifted out of place under the continuous deluge. Four feet of water flooded the houses at Twizel Mill and Twizel Bridge. Fortunately the mill workers at Heatherslaw Mill took speedy action as the river gained speed and height. They managed to use the water-powered winch to hoist over 500 bags of grain up to the second floor before the flood waters burst through the lower doors and windows, thus averting a huge loss.

The Pease Burn 'washout' occurred when the River Eye diverted its course to find the easiest route to the sea. It undercut the railway line north of Penmanshiel. (National Railway Museum, York. Collection NRM. No. 59/91)

Opposite: When Syphon Bridge collapsed near the Penmanshiel Tunnel, the debris rolled onto the main line railway. (Margaret Squires Collection)

From 10 a.m. Thursday 12 August

Reports came in of the sighting of an 'elephant's trunk' reaching from the sky near Seahouses. This was in fact a water spout or tornado, a particularly rare weather phenomenon in our neck of the (flooded) woods.

A harbinger of the floods to come occurred on the main line railway at Chathill railway station that morning. Driver Magee from Gateshead was in charge of the 12.24 p.m. express from Newcastle to Edinburgh when he noticed that much of the ballast for the track had been washed away. He signalled to Mr T.W. Robson, the Chathill Station Master, who in turn summoned the rail gangs to the line immediately. Following their inspection, the line was closed temporarily at 3.20 p.m. and was reopened in under two hours.

Small landslips caused by the excessive field run-off were the principal cause of blocked railway lines at first. Soon the flood would be raging so hard that it also took many bridges with it. (Margaret Squires Collection)

The southern express, which had been held up just north of Chathill, was lucky to be set free on its way, as the line behind it, between Scremerston and Goswick was also now seriously flooded. This same train also managed to escape a small land slip just south of Chathill. In a space of fifteen hours, the Edinburgh District Control Office for the Railways received over eighty reports of mishaps on the line.

Relief Station Master for Grantshouse, George Gowland, gave this harrowing account after returning to the station, having discovered that the line ahead and behind the railway station was cut off completely:

> *I looked towards the railway when I observed one of the bridges was falling down. It seemed to come down slowly at first, then with a rush, all the masonry fell into the seething water below.*

The River Tweed had by now burst its banks and very real concerns were being raised over the safety of the huge aqueduct of the Royal Tweed Bridge over the river at Berwick upon Tweed as logs and other debris piled up against the bridge supports,

Horsley Bridge, also known as the Free Kirk Bridge No.133, collapsed when her embankments were swept away, leaving her rails swinging in open air with no support. (Margaret Squires Collection)

The force of the water can only be imagined when you view the destruction left in its wake. This is another view of Horsley Bridge No.133. (Margaret Squires Collection)

literally damming the river and creating a huge strain on the structures as the pressure from the rising flood water hammered at the viaduct.

As a precaution, Berwick Bridge was closed to traffic from 10 a.m. on 13 August to 10 a.m. on 14 August. The lower reaches of Ord were by now under 15ft of water, cars and lorries were abandoned and residents of the houses in the affected area were rescued by salmon cobble.

Rainwater inches deep swept down into Tweedmouth, flooding homes along Main Street, necessitating the call out of the fire brigade to pump cellars; even the old, venerable and worthy hand-drawn fire pump from Tweedmouth Station – dated 1859 – was brought out, dusted off and used to pump out flooded cellars.

Thirty-two bus loads of day trippers were stranded overnight. Berwick was virtually cut off when Castle Drive, Castle Terrace, the Great North Road and Paxton Road all became impassable to traffic. Further, Main Street Tweedmouth, Dock Road, Main Street Spittal, Shielfield Terrace, Caledonian Road and Osborne Road were all either flooded or carried great quantities of water. Part of the railway

An aerial view of the River Tweed, flooded over the low-lying valley. Here you can see one abandoned fishing shiel and its tower; the next tower's shiel had been destroyed and swept away. (Margaret Squires Collection)

The Royal Scotsman seen here on the Royal Border Bridge had only just resumed its non-stop service from London Kings Cross to Edinburgh Haymarket when the entire East Coast Main Line would be shut down for eleven weeks. (Lawson Wood Collection)

Lorries were abandoned as the rivers flooded all access roads into Berwick and Tweedmouth and drivers had to wade waist deep to get clear. (Margaret Squires Collection)

embankment at Hud's Head subsided and the boundary wall to the railway bridge at Shielfield Terrace also collapsed. There were numerous slips at the cliffs at Magdalene Fields and there was a partial collapse of the Quay Wall including damage to the sewer outlet.

It was recorded that 4.606in of rain fell within the Burgh Walls. At the end of the day, the Burgh Council would be inundated with claims of hardship. There were twenty-nine cases in Berwick, twenty-nine flood distress cases in Glendale, thirty-two in Belford and a further sixty-five cases in Norham and the Islandshires.

At Whiteadder Bridge, or Canty's Bridge, on the Berwick to Kelso road, the Whiteadder overflowed its banks – as usual – but this time swept away three bungalows complete with furniture down the river. Some of the occupants sought shelter with Mrs Cameron at the Corporation Arms. A normal account of the time told of home owners going to respond to a knock on their door, only to open it to a rush of flood water. The knock had been from a flood-buoyed tree trunk.

> *We heard a terrific roar* [said Mrs Cameron] *and we wondered what had happened, we ran outside and found the bridge down. We tried to get in touch by phone to Berwick but telegraph posts and wires had been brought down to the ground.*

Apparently, a huge tree buoyed by the flood waters had crashed into one of the buttresses, damaging it so much that it had collapsed. Inside the pub, conditions worsened, the cellars had flooded, the beer barrels jostling for space amidst other flood water debris and two feet of water was in the kitchens. One of the residents in a nearby bungalow had a miraculous escape. Mr David Buglass decided to evacuate his bungalow when there was a major landslide adjacent to his property, caused by the amount of rainwater coming off the fields. Taking his wife and young family into their car, he set off to drive over the bridge up to Gainslaw. Next day he told a Berwickshire News reporter:

> *I had driven my car onto the bridge and was proceeding to cross it when suddenly I observed that the railings just ahead disappeared down into the river. Realising that the bridge was down, I quickly reversed and got back on to the roadway again. It was fortunate that I noticed the railings in my headlights when I did.*

An aerial view of where the Whiteadder Bridge, or Canty's Brig as it was known locally, used to be. A large tree had struck one of the buttresses and the bridge collapsed shortly after. (Margaret Squires Collection)

When Canty's Bridge collapsed, David Buglass and his family had a narrow escape when they almost drove into the river, attempting to escape from their ruined home. (Margaret Squires Collection)

His neighbour, Mr R.R. Yellolly, later told his fellow Rotarians of how he had been warned by Jack Hunter to get out of his bungalow as quick as possible as three of the nearby bungalows had just been swept into the river. He told of how he, his wife and young daughter left the house into 'great sheets of rain' and how he heard 'a great roaring and tearing sound, then a final crash . . . that was Canty's Bridge falling.' Thirty people from the farm were housed at High Cocklaw and another fifteen were housed at Jack Hunter's farm at Lilliestead. As well as the Whiteadder Bridge being down, the bridge at Fairney Flats was swept away and two landslides also blocked the road in the same vicinity.

Whiteadder or Canty's Bridge had been opened on 1 May 1868 during the annual Riding of the Bounds ceremony; the previous bridge had been built in 1834. Continuing flood waters over the prior sixty years had seen at least another six bridges over the same spot built in a variety of wood or stone, the wooden ones having generally faired better. A triple Bailey Bridge would be used at Canty's for many years to come, much longer than was originally anticipated. The Corporation Arms has now been renamed Canty's Brig and just as recently as 2001, cellars were flooded and a landslide once more blocked the road.

Others residents from the abandoned bungalows sought comfort with Mr and Mrs Mabon in their house at New Mills, but this was short lived as the river steadily rose and the thirty or so evacuees had to retreat to the second floor where they were later rescued and taken to High Cocklaw farm where Foster Wells and his wife made them comfortable until the Friday morning.

Recently married farm owner, sixty-five-year-old Jack Mabon, was the last to be pulled from his house, none the worse for his ordeal he said, 'I never want to have such an experience again. I have never known anything like it.' Reviewing a list of possessions lost in the flood by the Mabons, there were a variety of good quality fishing tackle including Hardy reels. There were also two accumulators of the Lisson type of three-valve, battery model wireless radios. These items are just a point of interest in times gone by. The Mabons lost everything including their home, but thankfully their lives were spared.

Mr W.V. Ross, from Hutton Mill House, his wife, daughter Anne and brother-in-law Jack Hattle, also sustained serious loss. The real threat came between six and eight o'clock that evening. When they saw the river rising, they lifted their carpets from

Mills received the brunt of the damage by the rising flood waters. Hutton Mill at Paxton was no exception, being virtually ruined when one of its walls collapsed. (Margaret Squires Collection)

Although Blackadder Bridge at Chirnside was still standing, the flood waters were over the ramparts and this low-lying bridge was closed to all traffic. (Lawson Wood Collection)

the bottom floor, but the river rose so quickly that they had to make for safety; the river rose to the second storey in a matter of only two hours. Mr Ross lost all his poultry and practically everything in the house was damaged, as well as the house. Mr Hattle's garage and motor lorry were washed away – the lorry was later detected in the mill stream. They spent the rest of that night at Broadmeadows, and on Friday moved to Berwick.

That day, it took twelve hours for a bus load of passengers to get from Edinburgh to Berwick. Mrs Jours from Ayton said:

> *It is only due to the clever driving of the driver that we were all still alive. I shall never forget the journey home. We tried all roads and it was when we arrived at Chirnside that it was decided that we should stay until daybreak. Some cottagers came across and asked us to go into one of the cottages. There was a roaring log fire and we were given tea and sandwiches. We left there at 5.30 a.m. and arrived at Berwick just before seven o'clock.*

In Duns, sixty feet of railway embankment was washed away at Littlefield and the sawmill at Kimmerghame collapsed under the weight of water and nothing remains of the mill. Mr Brown of Preston lost hundreds of pounds of timber when Broomhouse Bridge and Blanerne Bridge were swept away in the torrent. Wedding guests in Duns were forced back when the taxi returning them to Berwick couldn't

Campmoor Bridge on the Duns to Westruther road was also an early casualty of the flood when it collapsed swiftly, taking the road with it, thereby virtually severing all access to both towns. (Margaret Squires Collection)

get past Chirnside Bridge when workmen stopped them from going any further. They had passed whole hen huts floating in flooded fields surrounded by the bodies of hundreds of drowned chickens, sheep were huddled under trees barely able to find shelter, corn fields were flattened and hay stacks scattered everywhere.

The railway bridge at the east end of Greenlaw collapsed just minutes after a train passed over it. That part of the village was several feet deep in water for many hours, whilst locals battled to rescue the women from the houses. 'There was a rush to save my wife,' laughed Mr C.A. Frost, 'but no one wanted to save me and I had to wade through the water.' Considerable damage and loss of ingredients was done to the baker's shop belonging to Mr McGregor. Canteens arrived at lunchtime and arrangements were quickly made to transfer the homeless to billets at Duns High School later that day.

Reston was practically isolated with the major part of the village now under 3ft of water, as the river continued to rise and the drains unable to cope with the amount of runoff from the surrounding fields and railway line.

The road bridges at Heughhead Smithy and Coveyheugh collapsed and before dusk fell, a stretch of 40ft of the railway line on the London – Edinburgh route was left in mid-air when the bridge and 60ft of banking were swept away. The Howburn road was closed with over 4ft of water running along it, it would take another three days before the road link was opened and telephone lines repaired.

The crops belonging to Messrs Scotland were literally washed out of the ground. Mr Marshall at Waulk Mill in Reston lost three hen houses and forty-five hens, and although his house in the low-lying haugh of the River Eye was completely surrounded by water, he stayed put with his wife, aged mother and family of four. At Reston Mill, Mr Sherlaw lost forty hens and all his farm buildings. At nearby East Reston, Mr Inglis lost 140 hens, his crop of oats and potatoes were swept away and a haystack washed away down the river to further dam the stream at Ayton.

In Swinton, many houses were now flooded and the occupants seeking refuge with friends more fortunate than themselves. Most of the roads were rendered impassable and it was feared that all of the crops were ruined. Forty cattle were stranded on a hillock in Coldstream, the Market Square flooded for the first time and houses evacuated with the flood water rising higher than the last great flood of 1831.

The Leet and the Tweed sent flood water raging along Dovecote, Duke Street, Leet Street and Market Street. Canoeists helped to rescue personal possessions from the downstairs properties hit by the flood waters. Unfortunately for the Burgh, the water

The road bridge over the River Eye at the southern approaches to Reston was quickly swept away by the torrent. The gravel from the river bed was deposited feet deep over many of the low-lying agricultural fields. (Margaret Squires Collection)

These two bridges at Coveheugh in Reston were quickly swept away by the gathering flood waters, as the embankments were eroded by the swirling waters. (Lawson Wood Collection)

Coveyheugh, soon after its collapse, with the main line railway tracks and sleepers still joined together, swaying over the River Eye torrent. (Margaret Squires Collection)

Water levels crept over one foot higher than they did in the great flood of 1831, quickly inundating Tweedside and flooding Market Street in Coldstream. (Margaret Squires Collection)

Bridge and Border Marriage House, Coldstream
(Bridge built by Smeaton, 1766)

These two views of Coldstream Bridge before and during the flood, give a better appreciation of the amount of water which was moving down the Tweed valley system that fateful day on 12 August. (Lawson Wood Collection)

When Millburn Bridge fell, it spelled disaster for the first of two returning buses from a day's outing to Portobello. Here the bus, driven by Bob Grant, has just been pulled out of the hole in the road. (Margaret Squires Collection)

pumping station was now completely underwater and it would be another thirty-six hours before water was available to the properties in the town and when it did come back, all drinking water had to be boiled first.

Coldstream Bridge was still safe but the small spillway and weir were now a raging torrent with rapids carrying tons of logs into the bend of the river where they piled up further restricting the water flow and speeding up the spate. Water levels were so high that it had almost reached the top of the arches supporting this huge historic cross-border bridge.

When Millburn Bridge collapsed at three o'clock in the morning, things took a rather more serious turn as a bus with parents and children from Cranshaws crashed down into the water. Returning from a day out to Portobello, the bus and its twenty-five passengers were flung into the maelstrom when the bridge was swept away from underneath them. They were fortunately quickly rescued and given first aid by the passengers from the second bus from the outing. Eleven passengers and Bob Grant, the bus driver, were taken to Duns Knoll Hospital for treatment. The youngest person on the first bus was three-year-old Billy Graham, whose mother and sister were both injured in the crash. He was pulled out unscathed.

Jimmy Frizzle was in the second bus and told *Berwickshire News* reporters:

We started off from Edinburgh about 7.30 and had only gone a short way when one of the buses ran into a ditch and another bus had to be sent for. Weary and tired we passed a hotel about midnight and decided to ask for some tea, but we were refused by the hotel keeper, who said she was far too busy to deal with us. It was nearly three o'clock when we approached Millburn Bridge. I was in the second bus and we were just about to cross the bridge when someone who had managed to get out of the first bus stopped us.

Another of the passengers, Mr Hay, who farmed the land at Cockburn Mill, above Cumledge Mill, was less fortunate: he lost everything when his place received the full force of the water and swept everything before it.

For nine hours, Mr and Mrs Robert Welsh, their three-year-old child and a friend were marooned on the roof of their house at Abbey St Bathans, saved by breeches buoy just minutes before the house collapsed from underneath them. It was five o'clock when the police in Duns received word that they were stranded and in real difficulty. Rescue teams tried in vain with boat and ropes and things were getting desperate.

The Main Street in Ayton was quickly awash when the River Eye level rolled over the bridge and up the street, meeting flooding rainwater as it poured down the hills towards the crossroads. (Margaret Squires Collection)

These two photographs by a police photographer, show just how devastating the flooding around Mr Welsh's house was and how close he and his family came to being lost. (Margaret Squires Collection)

The buildings were crumbling and the family had had to move into the roof space. Mr Welsh watched in despair as the flood waters carried away his car and plucked furniture from the crumbling ruin of his house. A former German POW tried to swim with a line to the family several times, but was beaten back by the strength of the river. Nearing exhaustion, he told reporters that he was formerly in the German Navy and was a 'swimmer', having done similar rescue work in the past. His actions will be long remembered by eye witnesses.

Word was sent to Berwick & Eyemouth Coastguards and finally three teams of men managed to reach them around 3 a.m., my father, Robert Wood, included. Lines were fired across by rocket, the men on the roof attached them to the telephone bracket on the chimney post. Twenty miles from the sea, the Coastguards rescued them by breeches buoy. Similar scenes were enacted by the Burnmouth Coastguards at Allanton. The team were transported by army trucks, with the rocket apparatus manned and fired by one of the last 'Greenses' fishermen from Berwick, Robert 'Nagus' Crombie.

The now swollen River Eye was battling against extremely high tides and the harbour at Eyemouth was completely awash, housekeepers were evacuated with the rising tide. Those fishing boats still tied up in the harbour were moved to safer areas and double-moored, some boats were moved out and along the coast into less susceptible harbours , others were tossed onto the pier as if they were toys and not weighing the fifty tons which they actually were. Those fishing boats still at sea were

The water level had reached the second floor of Dundee House opposite Weatherhead's Boatyard, Black's Tea Room at the other side of the river was awash and the town was at a standstill. The flood waters raged down the cut and over the sluice gates, which soon became jammed with log debris. (Barbara Wood)

Clearly, the central arch on the Eyemouth Branch Line was swept away when the waters scoured away the base of the tower, causing its collapse. It would be ten months before the line could be used again. (Lawson Wood Collection & National Railway Museum, York. Collection NRM 05/02 No. 126/1/64)

In the path of the spate, the old wooden bridge at the bottom of the Smiddy Brae in Eyemouth (replaced by the 'Silver Bridge') was soon to be just more firewood collected on the beach. (Lawson Wood Collection)

warned not to visit the port until the danger had passed. Log debris was now some 15ft high, lodged against the sluice gates and overflowing onto the middle pier.

The central arch of the railway viaduct on the Eyemouth Branch line was undermined by the scouring action of the flood waters, collapsed and swept away. Fortunately the rail girders were not dislodged and were able to be further secured by wedges and ties.

Within the boatyard, a newly launched fishing boat for Jock Fairbairn was placed back up on its stocks and another new boat's hull, still under construction, ended part way up the banking. Thankfully the boatyard workers – at great risk – were able to attach strong ropes and chains to stop her being carried out to sea. One of the locals recalls that Mrs Weatherhead took her flooded piano apart piece by piece, cleaned it, reassembled it and it still played a fine tune!

The houses behind the boatyard at what used to be called Bridgend, were inundated with over 6ft of water on the ground floor. Mr Swanston, the occupier of the end house, said they salvaged as much as they could before the doors burst open and they had to seek refuge on the second floor. The other occupants were James White and Mrs Rae and family, all were rescued by ladder from the upper windows. The flooding was so bad along the harbour front that boxes of fish ready for transport to the markets of Leith and Manchester had to be loaded through to Church Street and a hole had to be knocked in the large wall around the yard to facilitate this.

Whilst this was bad enough in Eyemouth, the same scene was being enacted all the way up into East Lothian and across the Borders. In Haddington, Provost R.L. Fortune, accompanied by Mr W.C.M. Third, the general inspector for the Department of Health, and Mr J.J. Robertson MP, Under-secretary of State for

NUNGATE BRIDGE AND ABBEY CHURCH, HADDINGTON   A 2780

The normally peaceful Tyne quickly overflowed its banks and flooded the Nungate area of Haddington. (Lawson Wood Collection)

Locals watched in amazement from the bottom of the brae as the flood waters decimated the boatyard and steadily rose up the sides of the nearby buildings. One of the wooden buildings at the boatyard collapsed and was swept out to sea, a retaining wall was swept away and a new forty-ton fishing boat (LH 262) destined for Fisherrow was lifted by the flood tide and deposited on the quay. It would have to be launched for a second time! (Margaret Squires Collection)

These two views of Weatherhead's boat building yard show the constriction at the mouth of the 'cut' and the damage caused to the yard itself. In the background, the old wooden footbridge is no longer standing and the railway is at a standstill. (Margaret Squires Collection)

The railings on the concrete road near the sluice gates were bent parallel to the ground by the weight of the dunnage coming down the river. The water main along the quayside also burst and, whilst water was all around, there was no drinking water to be had in lower Eyemouth. (Margaret Squires Collection)

Scotland, visited the flooded area of his constituency to inspect the damage. Mr Robertson stressed that all appropriate Government Departments were prepared to do everything they could to assist local organisations in the relief of distress and he paid particular tribute to the excellent spirit that was being shown by those affected by the flooding, and to the manner in which they were taking their extreme difficulties.

The surrounding area of the river was usually inundated at some time or other, but now there was no telling where the river ended and the roads began. The deluge continued to be heavy along the whole length of the Tyne Valley and indeed, the rainfall at the source of the river's tributaries was so much heavier up in the Lammermuir Hills. These quickly flooded the Tyne and it overflowed its banks between three and four o'clock that morning. At the height of the flood, the River Tyne was approximately half a mile wide between Amisfield West Gate and the Town House.

Water flowed into the East Gate end of town and quickly inundated all of the buildings there. Most of the residents were taken by surprise due to the speed of the rising flood. Priority was the safety of the residents and most had to abandon all of their personal possessions.

The inhabitants along the Waterside and Nungate were in the worst peril, but this quickly spread along the Ford Row where some women had to be rescued through their upstairs window and carried by piggyback to dry land. (G.W. Day, Photographer, North Berwick)

One resident at St Martin's Gate found that eleven of his hens had perished and wasn't too amused when one local wag suggested that he should have kept ducks!

The Bermaline Mills and the Mill House suffered badly. Church Street, St Anne's Place and the Sands were all underwater, the old bowling green was a sheet of water and Tyne House near the Waterloo Bridge ended up on an island all by itself. The flood waters crept in with burglar-like stealth necessitating the speedy evacuation of all affected premises.

That evening, the water touched Home House garden wall and a large number of rats driven from their riverside holes were seen trying to save their lives by resting at the edge of the water. Their presence was, however, discovered by a band of local boys who, wading along under the wall, carried out an exciting and successful hunt. Come Friday there was no space for boy or rat!

In a report drafted by the Haddington Burgh Surveyor, it was reported that 149 dwelling houses were inundated, of which forty-four were rendered totally unfit for human occupation. About 460 persons were living in these houses and sustained damage to their belongings. In addition around ninety business premises including fifty-nine shops were flooded, approximately ten tons of foodstuffs were damaged by flood water and were either destroyed or disposed of by the Salvage Department of the Ministry of Food.

Following the flood, the Fire Service carried out sixty-four special services, which involved over 540 man hours and included pumping out cellars and washing out houses and business premises. Both cemeteries were flooded and St Martin's Old

Army trucks had to be brought in to help shift residents from the worst affected areas to the temporary accommodation in the Town Hall. (East Lothian Council Library Service)

When the Tyne overflowed in Haddington, it covered much further than ever before with over 149 houses and fifty-nine shops inundated by the flood. (East Lothian Council Library Service)

Kingside where the Whitecalder Water washed away large sections of the road at an unprotected bend. (G.W. Day, Photographer, North Berwick)

Burial Ground was also under water. Damage was also done to walks, layers, headstones and boundary walls around all the churchyards.

The footbridge over the Mill Lade at East Haugh and the Stevenson Footbridge over the river in the West Haugh were swept away. The railings and stone cope over the Mill Lade at the entrance to the Distillery Maltings were wrecked and a number of other footpaths and roadways received considerable damage. Sheaves of straw littered the footbridge at Preston, below East Linton, and dozens of sheaves were retrieved from the Mill Lade at Tyninghame.

In a field at Ormiston, occupied by gardener James Dickson, the workings of the old meadow pit gave way beneath the water. A hole about forty yards long and ten yards wide was created and through this the water rushed into the old workings from the fields flooded by the overflowing Tyne and Bellyford Burn. 'It was an amazing sight to see the cataract of water rushing into the hole at the far end of this fall,' he said. The spectators had to keep well back as other caverns began to form around the periphery of the large collapse.

Danger to the adjoining fields was feared as the water, now in the old mine workings, may have swept away the supports underneath. The waters rushed into the old Limeylands Pit, but this fact probably saved Ormiston Colliery; thankfully the men were alerted and made their way to safety through the Winton Mine. All the Limeylands miners were dispersed to other pit workings whilst their pit was out of action. Extra men from Newbattle were brought in to help pump out the mine workings.

Bridges down or impassable by the end of the day in the Haddington district

Jack Robertson breaking down the wall beside the Tyne to try and help drain the flooded areas back into the river basin. (East Lothian Council Library Service)

included Mains Hall; Coldale; Kingside; Whittingehame; Lint Mill; Barley Mill; Spilmersford by Pencaitland; Aikengall; Stottencleugh and Humbie Mains.

It was agreed that Provost R.L. Fortune would launch an immediate appeal to help those unfortunate persons affected by the flood. However, it was recognised that this fund could nowhere reach the sums needed to help those in need. With that in mind, representation was sent to Lord Provost Andrew Murray in Edinburgh. On this advice, Lord Provost Murray invited representatives of the affected areas to attend a meeting in the City Chambers, Edinburgh, on 19 August.

The Town Council agreed unanimously in an emergency meeting, subject to the approval of the Department of Health, to expedite the present building programme, in order to house the homeless families from the floods. Over 100 displaced persons were by now living in the Town Hall and the council were responsible for supplying all of their needs, including meals. Sixteen Cruden Houses were allocated immediately and will be ready by the end of the year at Lynn Lea Avenue in the Nungate.

Mr and Mrs David Ramage at Sandy's Mill on the Tyne, three miles east of Haddington, had to evacuate the mill around 10 p.m., unable to do anything about rescuing or releasing any of the farm animals. Returning the following afternoon, he was to discover that all his pigs had drowned except one, which was found two days later and several miles away. Two horses and a cow also manage to survive, although the water had been at least a foot higher than the cow's head! Three carts from the mill were never found again, but his lorry was discovered several hundred yards away with a broken axle. All his crops were ruined, his chickens and pullets drowned, but his two geese and twenty ducklings appeared quite happy at the state of affairs.

Biel House, owned by Rear-Admiral and Mrs Brookes, was opened to flooded families and campers within the immediate area. Police rescued a troop of girl guides at Broxmouth Park as their camp had been in direct line of the outlet from Spott Lake Reservoir, which it was feared may also burst its banks. Householders at Brand's Mill were also evacuated as a precautionary measure and the sluice gates were opened to relieve the pressure in the dam.

A later report would show that much of the flooding of Haddington is attributed to the construction of various weirs and dams on the Tyne which effectively lowered the banks that would have kept the water from overflowing low lying sections. There are five weirs in Haddington Parish alone and another three within a mile or two. But for these weirs, the river would have dug its channel deep enough naturally to carry ordinary flooding and each successive flood would have prepared the river bed for a greater flood. This was not the case however and it would be subsequently an ongoing problem in the Parish. It was noted that the water level at the Hopes Reservoir rose 12ft during the flood and only 6in above the sluice gates, therefore showing that the dam actually saved much of the low-lying ground from even greater damage, but had it been already full, then the results could have been catastrophic.

Several houses in Garvald were inundated when the Papana Water overflowed. Two families were rendered homeless and all were helped by the monks from Nunraw Abbey who supplied them with firewood and milk as well as providing dry clothing and bedding at the Abbey. The Papana Water hadn't been known to flood in living memory and it was sheer luck that no greater damage was caused. Seafield Farm owned by Dunbar Town Council was under several feet of water and helpers came from miles around to rescue the remaining pig stock which hadn't already perished and relocate them to a temporary piggery at Rosebank House.

When the Biel Burn burst its banks south of the Maltings, it made a short cut towards the sea by means of the new British Malt Products factory and the racing stables of George Boyd and West Barnes House. The flood waters hit twenty houses and fifteen families had to find alternative accommodation with relatives and friends, only one family needed to be re-housed and were initially placed in the Corn Exchange in Dunbar, where hot food was supplied to them by Dunbar V.A.Ds. The Town Clerk Mr W.S. Brown, accompanied by the Burgh Surveyor of Dunbar, Mr D.W. Murdoch, inspected the damage and flooded fields at the mouth of the Biel and made all arrangements for emergency relief.

Twenty racehorses had to be set loose by their trainer Mr George Boyd in case they were drowned. One of the horses, named 'Wellington Boots' and owned by Frank Usher from Dunglass, was swept away and later rescued after it had made its way ashore after being sucked under a humpbacked bridge and swept out to sea. Mr Boyd from West Barnes was in tears as he saw some of the horses carried off in the deluge, whilst others were trapped in their stalls, along with eleven stable lads who had to be lowered hot food through a hole in the stable roof. Working with his men in water chest deep, they tugged and pulled the other horses to safety. Thankfully all the horses survived.

Sadly things didn't have a happy ending at Powderhall Racecourse in Edinburgh. G.R.A. officials were unable to rescue many of the greyhounds and fifty-two dogs died when the Waters of Leith burst their banks and flooded all of the low-lying area. Two of the leading race track dogs in Scotland – Gold Deposit and Clan Cameron – were rescued but Pilton Pilot, another famous dog, was sadly drowned.

Tyninghame was overcome by the flooding Tyne which virtually destroyed the Mill. The heavy gates at the entrance were forced open and the yards were inundated by tree trunks and other debris. The Tyninghame Estate was flooded to a depth of several feet, cutting off the Tyninghame to North Berwick road. The occupants, Mr and Mrs Blyth, their infant child and Mr Blyth's parents, had to flee for safety around midnight and had to be settled in a vacant undamaged house in the village after spending an uncomfortable night with a relative at Tyninghame.

At East Linton, the severity of the rainfall pouring into the Tyne created a spectacular waterfall over the Linn Rocks under the Tyne Bridge. This sight had never been witnessed before by even the oldest inhabitants. The oat flour mill and saw mill were all but washed away, shops were flooded and the furniture store received major damage. All of the garden produce belonging to Mr Tom Watt was also swept away. Parts of Phantassie Farm were flooded and the market garden at Knowes Mill was swept asunder. The bridge over the Tyne below Hailes Farm leading to the Old Hailes Castle was also swept away and a double-decker bus driver, trying to avoid the flooded roads, got his bus stuck under the railway bridge.

Cumledge Mills after the flood water subsided. You can clearly see the water level up the side of the workers' houses. (Margaret Squires Collection)

Serious damage was done by flooding in the Stenton district near Dunbar, when the raging torrent swept down Pressmennan Loan and drastic action was taken to prevent the flood destroying the cottages from the lower Rood Well. Both the Ruchlaw Water (Sauchet) and the Whittingehame & Biel Water rose to unknown levels, overflowing their banks and destroying all crops in their path. The residents in Biel Mill Lodge were rescued in the nick of time by a group of volunteers, including a number of Boy Scouts, organised by Biel House. Those residents who had been away for the day were unable to return to their homes and had to stay with relatives or neighbours unaffected by the flood.

Cumledge Blanket Mills at Preston near Duns, one of the largest in Scotland, was rendered inoperable by a wall of flood water 7ft in height which completely overwhelmed the mill and the forty-two houses which surrounded the company.

The river Whiteadder was seen to burst its banks at five o'clock, but the locals had little chance to move furniture before the wave of water hit them and they scrambled for safety to the upstairs rooms. By eight o'clock, the houses were marooned and residents were signalling for help by torch-light from their upstairs windows. Looking out, they could see those more unfortunate than themselves – where houses, farm buildings and livestock were washed away. The flooding had started to lessen by ten o'clock but it was only until dawn of the next day that the true severity of the situation presented itself.

The water by now was only a foot deep, but mud and tree debris was piled high against the buildings. The brick built houses of the Misses Foreman had only the roof and gable ends standing, the centre walls and all of their contents swept away by the wall of water. Seventy-year-old William Robinson returned to where his house once stood, but nothing remained. Mr and Mrs Hunter and their Australian relatives who were unfortunately staying with them also lost all of their belongings.

Sixty-five-year-old Miss Isabella Simpson was brought to safety just before her house was swept away in the torrent. Cumledge Mills were started in 1854 by Mr William Laidlaw, the grandfather of Mr William Laidlaw, the director of the Mills when they were struck. Ashen-faced he said that it would be years before the mill would get going again, if at all. He gave special congratulations to the Ayton telephone exchange operators – Misses Jean and Mary Inglis – on the expeditious way in which they dealt with the big demand for long distance calls by officials and press men.

Mr and Mrs McIvor had watched in horror from their upstairs rooms, as the walls of their house were gradually undermined. Thankfully the water subsided before they

Mr James Cowe, the Works Manager, is seen here viewing the destruction of part of the Mill. The interiors were layered in silt and muddy water. (Margaret Squires Collection)

the aftermath of the inundation left the homes thick with mud, carpets ruined and furniture unusable. The water mark to the top of the ground floor windows and doors can clearly be seen. (Margaret Squires Collection)

Opposite: Buildings collapsed and stock was ruined under the rising sea of mud which destroyed Cumledge village and the blanket mill. (Margaret Squires Collection)

Margaret Squire's parents' house suffered major damage during the flood when the corner and gable end were undermined by the scouring action of the gravel laden water. They would receive no compensation from the relief fund. (Margaret Squires Collection)

The lower section of the bridge over the Whiteadder at Cumledge sustained enough damage to close the road and thus thwart rescue attempts from Duns at the height of the flood.
(Margaret Squires Collection)

were lost, but they watched transfixed as the nearby Mission Hall lifted itself from its foundations and 'floated off like Noah's Ark', said Mrs McIvor.

Police from Duns tried to reach the village about ten o'clock but part of the small bridge was washed away and the rest of the road undermined. It would be many hours before the council could muster help, food provisions and fresh water to help these hapless villagers whose livelihood was destroyed in a single day of rain.

The River Eye had burst its banks at Burnmouth and the railway line was now under 3ft of water, the river having made a new course for itself. Two hours later, two landslips further blocked the Eyemouth branch line and another landslide blocked both the north and southbound tracks of the main East Coast line at Marshall Meadows just to the north of Berwick. Further south into Northumberland, the railway line fared much better with only temporary flooding at Little Mill, Chathill, Belford stations and the line between Scremerston and Goswick. The only serious damage was the collapse of the bridge at Mindrum which blocked the Alnwick to Coldstream goods line.

North of Grantshouse, at 7.08 p.m., it was reported that bridges 124, 125 and 127 were swept away. Later on at 8.30 p.m., the Grantshouse Station Master called to report that bridges Nos 123, 126, 128 and 130 had collapsed, necessitating the re-routing of the Flying Scotsman from Kings Cross onto the 'Waverly Route' (Carlisle to Edinburgh portion).

Framed under the broken arch of the Whiteadder Bridge at Cumledge, the factory buildings can be seen in the distance with smoke coming out of the large chimney. Sadly the factory would close in the near future. (Bill Cormack)

Station staff at Grantshouse watched with dismay when the rising flood burst the banks of the River Eye and poured gravel and other debris over the railway track, blocking both lines of the East Coast Main Line. (Alastair Scott)

Mason's Bridge No.130, north of Grantshouse, was another casualty as the flood water continued its path of destruction along the east coast railway line. (Margaret Squires Collection)

Opposite: Harelawside Bridge No.123 was left with her rails swinging in open air above the swirling torrent of the River Eye. (Margaret Squires Collection)

Renton House Bridge No. 125 was similarly hit when her embankment was swept away, also leaving her rails dangerously exposed. (Margaret Squires Collection)

Unfortunately this was short lived as a landslide was reported on the down line between Borthwick Bank and Gorebridge and another landslide over both lines at Tynehead; thus the Waverly Route was also blocked to all rail traffic. Thereafter all rail traffic had to be diverted to the West Coast route through Carlisle to Carstairs and Edinbugh Haymarket West. The affected lines were:

Edinburgh–Berwick main line between Dunbar and Marshall Meadows
Edinburgh–Carlisle main line between Hardengreen and Galashiels
St Boswells–Kelso–Tweedmouth line between Sprouston and Carham
St Boswells–Reston line between Greenlaw and Reston
Jedburgh branch line beyond Bankfoot
Dalkeith branch line beyond Glenesk Junction
Peebles branch line
Polton branch line
Penicuik branch line
Lauder branch line
Eyemouth branch line
Haddington branch line
Gifford branch line

The London King's Cross to Edinburgh Waverly express was stopped at Tynehead with a blocked railway line and had to be rerouted via Carlisle. (National Railway Museum, York. Collection NRM No. 58/91)

This destruction by the forces of nature was unparalleled in all of British railway history. Of the stranded trains, only one lightly loaded passenger train was stuck in Berwickshire. This was the St Boswells to Reston train which could get no further than Chirnside. Passengers had no alternative but to stay on the train and get what sleep they could as no rescue was forthcoming until the next morning. The 10.05 Edinburgh Waverly to London King's Cross passenger train was stopped at Tynehead and a bus load of food was sent to ease the position of the passengers.

The 10.10 a.m. Edinburgh Waverly to St Pancras and the 10.37 a.m. Edinburgh to Leeds were combined and *The Queen of Scots* Pullman due to leave Glasgow Queen Street at 10.15 a.m. were all scheduled to detour via Carstairs with connections to and from Edinburgh. There were another three stranded goods trains, one each at Ayton, Reston and Cockburnspath. It would take considerably more time, effort and resources before these could move once more. In all, six locomotives were immobilised and this put further strain on the already stretched resources of British Rail.

The swing bridge at Blue Stone Ford was washed away and part of it now lay on the Hutton side of the river, still fixed to its standards. The wooden footbridge leading to it had also been swept away, while the middle of the paved ford was washed

A new 'lake' formed on the low-lying ground west of Ayton, when the Beanburn flooded. It was this lake that was seen as a major threat to the fishing village of Eyemouth. (The Scotsman Archive)

Railway engineers examine the top of the embankment above culvert No.146 to determine what should be done with the dammed water (excuse the pun). (Margaret Squires Collection)

out. The water at this point covered Nethermains Haugh to nearly 200yds in width, with all of the dykes and hedges having been washed away. The road leading to it from the Hutton side was also blocked and undermined. Todheugh Bridge on the River Whiteadder, near Edrom, was also washed away.

Eyemouth residents at this time were now informed of a new lake which had formed in the Eye valley west of Ayton when culvert No. 146 collapsed. Some 4 million tons of flood water was only held back by a now crumbling railway embankment. This mass of water continued to grow at an alarming rate throughout the rest of the week and come the following Sunday it was 1½ miles long and over 40ft deep. The railway embankment was 60ft wide and as water started to seep through, there were landslips on the drier Ayton side of the gorge.

Friday 13 August

Friday saw the Cumledge Mill residents attempting to dry off furniture on the surrounding debris. Mr Vallance discovered that the raging current had taken his car out of his garage over stone walls and deposited it in a tree over a hundred yards away. In the remains of the mill, machinery weighing many tons were lifted from their fixings and sockets on the floor, Floors had been ripped up, walls and roofs collapsed, half-ton bales of wool and oil drums were floating down the River Whiteadder as if they were match-wood and what was left was now covered in reddish mud. £24,000 of machinery and 500 spindles lay rusting.

The sun was shining and a splendid rainbow could be seen arching low over the River Eye and stretched over the new lake at Prenderguest. Showers also fell during the day causing more anxiety to this waterlogged south-east corner of Scotland. Meteorologists estimated that almost 6in of rain fell in the previous twenty-four-hour period, with at least half of that falling in the six hour period between 1 p.m. and 7 p.m. on the Thursday.

Solely through the efforts of a massive influx of railwaymen, the Waverly Route and St Boswells–Kelso–Tweedmouth lines were reopened to passenger and freight

This page and next: Residents at Cumledge Mill started the lengthy process of collecting up any items worth salvaging and try to dry out their belongings. (Margaret Squires Collection)

Mr Vallance's car was eventually discovered and all hands were called on to extract the stricken vehicle from the mud and tree debris. (Margaret Squires Collection)

Massive collections of steel reinforcing rails and sleepers were collected at various depots for immediate transportation to the affected areas. It was only through this massive combined effort that work was able to progress so speedily. (National Railway Museum, York. NRM 17/02 No.126/35/64)

traffic by 2.15 p.m. Although the double line could not be fully restored immediately, there was suitable provision for all traffic to pass safely, but at a much reduced speed. The upshot of these immediate repairs was to ease the strain on the main East Coast line and allow for a much greater improvement and repair plan to be implemented. Whilst this work progressed, bus services would operate between all of the affected stations and closed sections of line.

News was only just starting to filter through from the outlying areas of the eastern Borders. The new 'lake' hit national headlines in every newspaper in Britain. Everyone waited with baited breath for the news which could either spare the fishing town of Eyemouth, or whether it would go under the estimated 30ft tidal wave which threatened to engulf the town. As in many disaster cases, Eyemouth attracted its fair share of thrill-seeking sightseers.

Over 50yds of Berwick Quay near the Berwick Salmon Fisheries Co. premises were severely damaged by the heavy river. One stretch of over 30yds completely broke away from the rest of the quay, leaving a gap of about two yards, while at another part, the quay caved in leaving a large crater. With each high tide, the gap became more pronounced until it became completely unusable.

Torn trunks and branches almost choked the River Eye where it flows into Eyemouth harbour and several huge trunks had been lifted by the raging waters of the Eye right over the quayside into Harbour Road, whose cobbled stones had been evenly dyed red with Berwickshire's soil left by the receding waters. The loss of livestock could not yet be reckoned along the local river valleys. (Margaret Squires Collection)

These three picture postcards were quickly produced by enterprising local photographer and pharmacist, Mr A. McIvor, to sell to a population hungry for such 'disaster scenes'. The local boarding houses which weren't flooded with water were now flooded with visitors. (Lawson Wood Collection)

AFTER THE FLOOD, EYEMOUTH. 13.8.48.   C6053

The lower reaches of Kelso were flooded, the River Tweed spread far and wide over the surrounding farmland. A huge log jam at Kelso Bridge stopped the spate dead and from there it spread out over the Springwood field on the corner at the bend of the river: there was now no corner! The Duke of Roxburghe at Floors Castle wrote:

> *I think the following facts are of interest and should be recorded as resulting from the disastrous storm which hit the south-east of Scotland on 12th August.*
>
> *The Tweed extended 3 feet 8 inches beyond and 6½ inches higher than the previous flood of 1831, which is recorded by a stone mark in the park here with the following inscription: 'Height of Flood, 2 p.m., 9th Feb,. 1831.' The rainfall recorded at Floors for the 24 hours 8 a.m. 12th August to 8 a.m. 13th August was 6.12 inches. When one realises that the previous maximum, recorded 117 years ago, was exceeded it is not surprising that the devastation caused was so violent and widespread.*

Riverside Street in Peebles was aptly named – it was now a river! Whilst the local schools were thankfully still on their summer recess, children were photographed playing in the 'new town rivers' up and down the Borders as the rainfall finally lessened. The maternity wing at Ardenlea Hospital in Peebles was also struck by the flood. Polish nurse Aline Rosenthal was marooned with fifteen babies. Fortunately she was able to take them upstairs in time, but it would be fifteen hours before she could be rescued by firemen. In the adjoining general wing of the hospital, patients were rescued by volunteers.

Clean up operations were soon underway at Harelawside Cottages, with residents rinsing off some of their goods in the flood water! (Margaret Squires Collection)

The Borders paper mills were similarly hit with extensive damage caused. Mr Hay, the manager at the Chirnside plant, made an offer to the employees to clear up the debris which would keep them off the Labour Exchange. At Edington Mills, south of Chirnside, owned by Messrs R.F. Bell and sons of Leith, the water level from the overflowing Whiteadder had reached the second floor at the height of the torrent.

Provost R.L. Fortune made the following appeal to the Editor of *Haddington Courier*:

> *Sir: As Provost of the Royal Burgh of Haddington, I wish to make a strong appeal for financial assistance for the many victims of the recent floods which have devastated several parts of our town (Distillery Park, Poldrate & Nungate being the worst hit).* (East Lothian Council Library Service)

Under the supervision of Dr Mitchell Innes, funds were withdrawn from the Chirnside Common Good Fund and food parcels supplied from the Red Cross stores for the families directly affected by the flood and whose homes had been lost. These

Other mills were also similarly hit by the flood. Chirnside Mill, seen in these before and after photographs, had to lay off most of its workforce after the flood and it would a be a few weeks before production was able to start once more. (Lawson Wood Collection)

families were now encamped in Chirnside new school. Dr Salem and Dr Ross Hair worked tirelessly to help the welfare of the stricken families. Berwickshire County Council had to revert to supplying water by lorry, stopping at houses in the local villages as all water main supplies had been cut, the machinery was unable to cope or damaged by the flood.

It was still the Earlston trades week and many local residents were still away on holiday, unaware that their homes are under three feet of water. When the Leader flooded this time, it flooded homes where it had never reached before, or since. It would be Saturday before the road was opened again, but gas, telephone and electric services would be unavailable for several more days. Beekeepers in Swinton lost all of their hives when the flood inundated the fields and the footbridges in Lauder were swept away.

The River Gala surged through the main streets of Galashiels causing thousands of pounds worth of damage to the mills. A weir was demolished and the football ground

Bill Cormack's motorcycle rests against the ruined Pease Bay Road where the River Eye cut a swathe of destruction down the valley. (Bill Cormack)

Opposite: *At South Renton Cottages, bed linen was soon hanging out to dry in the aftermath of the flood.* (Margaret Squires Collection)

Seventy-two-year-old Mrs William Dougal and her husband were rescued from their isolated farm house at Brockholes, Grantshouse, by a team of firemen tied to a rope stretched across the road, should they be swept away. Feared drowned, the two had managed to survive by standing on a table placed on top of a high bed. When rescue arrived, the water was lapping at their necks. (Margaret Squires Collection)

Many of the riverbeds and bankings would be reformed along the sides of the worst affected rivers. (Bill Cormack)

disappeared. The road bridge to Buckholm Mill was washed away and several others undermined. Tenants of the houses at Galafoot had to evacuate their homes by means of a plank stretched across from their second-storey windows to the railway embankment behind. The Ladhope Burn was now a river and had changed course to run along the railway line. Galashiels Ratepayers' Association launched a relief fund for townspeople whose property was lost or damaged by the flood waters.

Whilst some of the water level had abated due to the river finding alternate routes of dissipation, the railway station at Grantshouse was still cut off by about 3-4ft of muddy water and the railway embankment was now completely swept away. The railway line swayed crazily above the surging Eye Water. Finding the weakest link in the embankment, the water forced its way through and thenceforth to the Penmanshiel railway tunnel, from there into Pease Glen where it rushed towards the sea at Pease Beach, virtually destroying the Mill in its path. Eye-witnesses would say that the water level had risen to within almost four feet of the crown of the Penmanshiel tunnel.

The River Eye quickly found a new course when it burst its banks to the north of the Penmanshiel Tunnel. (Margaret Squires Collection)

The Pease Bay road was impassable due to landslides and the beach was piled up with wood. Great holes were washed out of the railway embankments while landslides occurred on the banks and in the cuttings, covering the entire double line in certain places.

Stone from the old Grantshouse Quarry would be used to reinforce the river bed of the Eye and a small Distress Fund was also organised in the village. In fact, much of the gravel which was swept onto the railway line and roads was reused to reinforce the new concrete embankments which were placed at strategic corners.

Saturday 14 August

A team of Royal Engineers and specialist drillers from Edinburgh abandoned the idea of siphoning the lake over the embankment as it was rising faster than the water could be released. All rail traffic was halted and the railway line was cleared as quickly as possible by the volunteer army of linemen and local farmers; the rails and sleepers

Work continued to reduce the weight on the embankment and to start works on a sluicing system to try and reduce the water pressure. (Margaret Squires Collection)

were lying at the foot of the 80ft embankment. Subsidence continued on the eastern side of the banking as water continued to seep through the collapsed culvert.

The need to reduce the pressure of the millions of tons of water held back was now paramount as Eyemouth and its population of 2,500 people lay in the path of this massive destructive force. Should it break through, a tidal wave would rush over the flooded fields and join the River Eye at Ayton. Plans were now drawn up for the total evacuation of Eyemouth harbour area. The Ale water tributary was already in full spate and this was adding to the pressure on the Eye.

The gorge itself is only 30yds wide in places and this would have the effect of speeding up the torrent of water into an even more destructive force. From there it would rush down the Eye valley and engulf the houses at the low-lying harbour level in the town.

Farm cottages in the path of the 'lake' were evacuated and all rail traffic was at a standstill with seven rail bridges and two road bridges swept away already in an eight-mile stretch of the countryside between Ayton and Cockburnspath. Police issued a statement appealing against pilfering, as it had been reported that some vacant properties had been looted.

The huge log jam over the sluice gates at the rear of Eyemouth Harbour attracted visitors from far and wide, as well as locals who helped to 'collect' the firewood. (Margaret Squires Collection)

Back in Cumledge, whilst the river level had now subsided, the residents took the opportunity to try and dry off more of their flood water-soaked furniture by placing it on top of the piles of river debris which was pushed up against their houses. Residents counted the loss: one man had his life savings of £120 lost when the trunk it was in was wept away, another local escaped from her house with only twopence!

A 30ft-wide crevasse was found in the Westruther to Duns road when the road collapsed after being undermined by the flood waters of the previous two days. Very real difficulties were now presenting themselves as land and rail routes were now almost completely cut off, telephone lines were down and emergency services were suffering difficulties in reaching the worst affected areas.

Saturday afternoon saw an amazing sight as hundreds of sightseers arrived by foot, bicycle and car to look at the devastation and gaze in wonder at the lake which had formed on Mr Douglas Lindsay's farm at Prenderguest.

Eyemouth saw similar scenes, despite warnings by the police that the town was likely to be lost due to the 'tidal wave of destruction'. Whilst many storms appear to take place in the dead of night, there was no denying the flood waters which cascaded over Eyemouth pier and quayside during midday.

Locals and visitors could only watch in awe at the massive destructive force and the sheer amount of water which was moving through the 'cut'. Crowds jammed the lower section of the Smiddy Brae to watch the muddy waters rushing past, filled with trees and other flotsam.

Sunday 15 August

The *Sunday Post* stated:

FIVE-MILE STRETCH OF WATER MAY SWEEP OVER EYEMOUTH
Workers' Day-And-Night Battle To Avert Disaster – 2000 Watch For Signal Rocket

Mr Arthur Woodburn, Secretary of State for Scotland, interrupted his holidays at North Berwick to visit the area and declared 'A State Of Emergency' for the eastern Borders villages.

Army trucks and jeeps were sent out into the area by orders of the Scottish Command and the Ministry of Transport approached the War Office to make available parties of Royal Engineers and sapper officers for the possible repair of road and rail bridges, should the deluge continue. Of paramount importance was to ease the terrific strain

Although the River Eye was still in spate, locals at the bottom of Brown's Bank or 'The Bane Mill Brae' were determined to try and dry off what articles they could. (Barbara Wood)

which would be placed on the communications network should the collapse continue. Named after Sir Donald Bailey, who developed them during the Second World War, Bailey bridges had already been delivered to a number of areas and were ready to be erected. Fortunately, the devastation occurred quite close after the war and National Service was still in place, allowing teams of engineers to be available immediately. By now twenty-one rail bridges in Scotland and eighteen bridges in Northumberland were either impassable or down. Thankfully the water level in the 'lake' had dropped several feet during the night and, whilst the alert was still in place and all necessary precautions were being taken, some of the water had found a way out through a nearby culvert into the River Eye. On the other hand, however, the red clay on the other side of the embankment had started to slip and an emergency inspection was carried out by the Chief Regional Inspector of Railways and Chief Engineer from Edinburgh.

3 a.m. Monday 16 August

The headlines of the *Daily Express* that morning announced:

BIG FLOOD – BARRIER IN DANGER –
2,500 Sleep As Waters Pile Up – Watchers Set To Warn The Town

Railway surface-men and two volunteers (wartime air raid wardens from Ayton) stood vigil should the waters break through the 300yd stretch of embankment most at risk. They were to telephone a warning to a waiting telephonist in Eyemouth; from there, a message would be flashed to the local Coastguard, A.D. Chalmers, who would warn the town by setting off an unprecedented four maroons to order the evacuation of the town. Ayton was to be warned by the old air raid siren which would whine the alarm. It was calculated that it would take eighteen minutes for the water to reach the areas most at risk and in that time men, detailed on night-and-day watch would race to houses in the lower parts of Eyemouth to assist families in reaching the surrounding hills. The Salvation Army was 'at the ready' to rush in supplies of bedding and other necessities. Everyone was hoping that if the flood did sweep down it would not clash with the high tides expected towards the end of the week. 'God knows what would happen to the fishing fleet,' one fisherman commented.

The Minutes of the Railway Executive with Sir Eustace Missenden (in the chair) included the following information:

> *Other bridges washed away or collapsed are at Duns and Greenlaw on the Berwickshire Line and near Humbie and Fountainhall and on the Eyemouth Branch. Berwick, Burnmouth, Chathill and Goswick stations were all flooded and there was a considerable number of land lines and flooding on secondary and branch lines. The non-availability of the East Coast route has necessitated a recasting of booked train schedules and an emergency passenger and freight service has been prepared.*

Stranded railway goods wagons had to be winched off the damaged tracks from the Chirnside Paper Mill branch line. They were lifted by steam crane onto the main line railway which ran overhead. (National Railway Museum, York. NRM 09/02 No. 126/17/64)

Tuesday 17 August

Despite more rain, the water level on the lake had not risen any more and the Earl of Home, Lord Lieutenant of Berwickshire toured the flooded areas. He was quoted as saying that it would be at least another few days before the danger had passed, as part of the embankment had subsided, but it was hoped that Eyemouth would still be spared from the deluge.

The gasworks manager, Mr R. Jones, and his neighbours, Mrs York and Mr and Mrs John Finlay and their young son, who live adjacent to Ayton Mill, had been ordered to evacuate their houses as a precautionary measure by the police. Mrs York however told the *Berwickshire News* reporter:

> *I am not going to leave the house, I am not frightened and if the water does rise it can come no higher than it was on Thursday or Friday. There are far too many heid yins gadding about the countryside in fine cars gliffin everybody. There is no need to fear and we are staying put here.*

In their first year of nationalisation, all of the resources at the disposal of the railways were needed to effect the immediate repairs of the damaged tracks. First on the list was the repair of the railway line between Tweedmouth and Galashiels to allow the train services to continue.

1948 had seen the resumption of the non-stop *Flying Scotsman* service between Edinburgh and King's Cross in London. This non-stop service would continue, but with an extended timetable of around forty-five minutes to accommodate the 25mph speed restriction imposed on the line between St Boswells and Tweedmouth. The first train that made it through was the *Flying Scotsman* which had left London King's Cross at 10 a.m. and gallantly steamed into Edinburgh Waverley at 3.51 the next morning!

Of the various trains which made the non-stop journey were Gresley locomotives of the A4 streamlined class, No.60029 *Woodcock*, which did at least four double runs, No.60012 *Commonwealth of Australia* and Nos 60022 *Mallard*, 60027 *Merlin*, 60028 *Walter K. Whigham* and the 60031 *Golden Plover*. These trains would run a total of seventeen non-stop journeys on the route of the *Flying Scotsman* during the emergency.

Wednesday 18 August

Bright skies lifted everyone's spirits, the water level had dropped in the lake and the embankment still held firm. Although the hazard appeared to have passed, the army engineers and signallers were still on standby, should a breach occur.

At the Chirnside Paper Mill, Mr Hay the manager reported good progress in the cleaning up and reconstruction of the plant. Steam had been raised in several of the engines and other machines had successfully been started for a short while to help them get run in.

All of the female labour had now signed on at the Labour Exchange and Mr Hay was very hopeful about having them all back to full work in a course of a few weeks and that all damage incurred there, could be rectified within two to three months.

However, the Earl of Haddington, convener of Berwickshire County Council, did not strike a hopeful note about Cumledge Mills, when he said that he thought it unlikely that the mills would ever open again. The Earl suggested that perhaps the men could be employed to help the farmers gather the crop as machinery was useless in the ruined fields.

Furniture lost by the householders was collected with the aid of the Ministry of Transport and it was stored in a central place – Chirnside School – until claimed by the owners. Flood victims Mabon and Penny were still contained in Chirnside School and spoke very highly of their treatment. Berwickshire County Council were still not able to find them alternative accommodation, but were hopeful that a house would be found soon.

Local postmen had a hard time getting to some of the rural areas due to so many bridges being down. Deliveries were expected to take at least thirty minutes to one hour longer than usual due to the long walks involved to some of the farm houses. However, delivery men commented that it was no worse a task than during the winter snows when they generally have to walk longer distances!

The flooded Cockburnspath Smithy and former slaughterhouse near Penmanshiel were now cleared of mud after a motor van was removed from the muddy debris, having been pushed into the premises by the flood, and the washed-out Burnside Road repaired. Pease Glen road was impassable due to land slippage and the ford and beach at the bottom of the Glen were also rendered unusable due to the amount of debris, logs and rubbish piled high.

The road bridge between Hoprig and Fernilea was damaged and rendered unfit for use, while the bridge between Stockbridge and Ecclaw collapsed. The Dunglass Estate power station was several feet under water at one time, but fortunately no serious damage ensued. The worst feature of this time which affected the small coastal hamlet of Cove was the lack of fresh water, as the storage tanks emptied and water pipes were still too damaged at Oldhamstocks Glen to effect a full repair.

Few houses were damaged in Oldhamstocks, but Mr Kosinski lost one hut with about twenty chickens in it. Some of the farm roads were badly damaged, especially at Stottencleugh and Woodlands. All the foot bridges were carried away and because of the damage to the road bridge at Hoprig, there is no traffic to Cockburnspath.

Further heavy rain raised some anxiety as the streams coloured and once more started to rise, but there was no further flooding. Harvesting had begun on a number of farms, but it was very heavy-going due to the condition of the soil. Many were using scythes once more, as much of the agricultural machinery could not be used.

St Abbs village escaped very lightly from the effects of the flood; only a wooden foot-bridge on the way to St Abbs Head had been swept away and a landslide at White Heugh had rendered the pathway impassable. The pathway leading to Coldingham Sands from the 'Shore' had been 'gutted' and all of the fishermen were still tired and weary from having to constantly bail out their small fishing boats every hour or so to keep them from sinking. The roadway down the sands was also badly hit and several of the beach huts at the bottom of the brae were damaged by water running with great force down the road off the surrounding steeply sloping fields.

Thursday 19 August

A week after the terrific floods devastated the Borders and Northumberland, a National Disaster Fund to relieve victims of distress was opened by Mr J.J. Robertson, Under-secretary of State. He said that appeals should be centralised and not allowed to spring up mushroom fashion. He emphasised that such a fund would benefit the whole of the flooded area, irrespective of any line of demarcation.

The fund, instigated by Lord Provost Murray from Edinburgh, would be distributed locally, where the need existed, by local committees who could act quickly and with local knowledge, while the general policy and direction would rest with an executive committee composed of the Lords-Lieutenant and the Convenors of Counties of all districts making claims against the flood. The fund did not aim to relieve national or local responsibility but to augment it, nor did it seek to meet the legal responsibility of individuals but sought to give that little extra which would turn four walls and roof into a warm, happy and cosy home.

Announcing that their Majesties King George VI and Queen Elizabeth had graciously sent a contribution to the fund, he concluded by asking, 'Will you follow this generous lead and send your donations to help these men, women and children, hardworking honest folk who, through no fault of their own, have lost in many cases everything and in every case something?' By the end of that day donations reached £2,716. However, other smaller funds still started.

It was agreed that all funds received in East Lothian, whether from the central fund or from any other source, should go into one account with the Bank of Scotland, Haddington Branch, and be administered by a committee known as the East Lothian Consultative Flood Relief Committee consisting of Lord Tweeddale, Lord Lietenant of the County as Chairman; Major Sir H. Broun-Lindsay, Convenor of the County Council; Provost Ross, Vice-Convenor of the County Council; Bailie John Robertson, Chairman of the County Welfare Committee; Provost R.L. Fortune and Treasurer George Murray of Haddington; Provost A.J. Manderson and Treasurer Major Mills of Dunbar; with Mr Thomas Gibb, County Clerk as Clerk and Mr J.L. Lochhead, County Treasurer as Treasurer. Authority was granted for the account to be operated on jointly by Provost Fortune and Mr Lochhead.

Meanwhile, the Cumledge Mill Distress Fund was receiving donations from many locals, including the children of Tiendhillgreen in Duns who raised £11 from an open air concert on the Bowling Green and a further £5 from the sale of refreshments. Supplies of large timber arrived at Ayton for the timbering of a channel prior to the construction of a sluice gate. Army engineers and specialist construction workers from Edinburgh were now working tirelessly to dig through the banking in a final effort to drain the lake. The first of the 'Mystery Tour' buses arrived by an enterprising Dunbar Bus Company. Passengers visited the 'lake' and Eyemouth Harbour where they were able to view the destruction and the dangerous levels of the River Eye at Ayton and Eyemouth.

Work continued at Eyemouth Harbour to clear away the debris and tree trunks which had been swept downstream, destroying everything in their path, including railway pilings and the wooden bridge just upstream of the harbour sluice gates. A huge 80ft trunk, which was lodged at the end of the quay, was finally removed by crane – 12ft at a time. Work at the sluice gates was stopped to give priority to the tree removal. (Margaret Squires Collection)

With the new sluice gates now in operation on the embankment, the water was steadily drained to ease the pressure and reduce the risk of collapse. (Margaret Squires Collection & Lawson Wood Collection)

Friday 20 August

Lord Provost Murray from Edinburgh visited Eyemouth, where he conferred with the acting Provost, Bailie James S. Collin, and the Town Clerk, Mr J.C. Muir, on arrangements for relieving the distress of flood victims. After the meeting held in the Town Clerk's offices, the group, accompanied by the Town Clerk of Edinburgh and the Chief Constable, visited the quayside where they inspected the barrier of ruined trees at the sluice gates.

Haddington's relief fund had by now realised £1,214, Haddington Town Council heading the list of donations by placing one penny per pound on the rates, which gave £150 immediately. An initial private donation of £100 was also handed in anonymously.

At the railway embankment at Prenderguest, the sluice gates and channel were finally completed in the late evening, having dug to 15ft from the lake, in readiness for the draining. Thankfully the water level was still falling steadily and farmers over the next weekend salvaged as much of the ruined crop as possible.

Mr W. Turnbull of Allanbank who was recorded by the BBC News Service at Allanton, however stated that he estimated his loss of stock, grain and pasture at around £1,000. Criticism was raised by Councillor A. Tait of Ayton about the length of time it had taken in dealing with the flood menace. He contended that local residents should have been kept more aware of the plans and subsequent danger should any of those plans failed. He said:

> *It is a scandal that nothing definite has been done. The water has been lying there for six days. Plenty of officials, even from the Home Office, have been running about the countryside in cars, but apparently doing nothing about it. First there was one plan, then another, and now another plan has been brought into use. It seems to have been a case of one department passing the buck to the other. The tension, especially amongst the older people, has increased, especially since the warning instructions about the evacuation of houses was issued. Much of this could be avoided if the authorities only keep the residents informed of what the position is from time to time. Personally I do not fear any serious flooding if the embankment does give.*

Interestingly, Mr Tait had his office and works at Ayton Mill, half of which was washed away when the river first overflowed its banks the previous week.

Shipbuilders, joiners and other workmen at the shipbuilding yard were all engaged over the weekend clearing away the hundreds of tons of mud left behind when the flood waters receded. Work started soon on the erection of another bridge at the bottom of the Bane Mill Brae. Thankfully a dredger, which was supposed to have left two weeks prior to the flood, was still moored at Eyemouth and was be used to clear the harbour of the remaining debris.

Engineers erecting one of the Bailey Bridges at East End Greenlaw. (Margaret Squires Collection)

Saturday 21 August

The first of the lorries arrived at Chirnside Old School with collected personal articles and furniture salvaged from the various riverbanks after the flood waters had receded. Accompanied by a local police officer, articles were recorded and laid out for identification by the former owners. Notice was placed in the *Berwickshire News* to summon people to identify their lost property.

Villagers turned out in their droves in Greenlaw to watch in wonder and admiration the assembly of the triple Bailey bridge, erected to replace the damaged road bridge at the east end of the village. The sappers from the R.E. training regiment from Elgin worked like trojans completed the job in only a couple of days, with the seventy-ton bridge spanning 120ft. It was estimated that the bridge would be in place for seven years. The Bailey bridge at the Shank, Kelso, which is 70ft long, was built in about seven hours under Army direction by civilian workers who began work at 8 a.m. and the bridge was completed at Kingside by 1 p.m. which was two hours ahead of schedule. A further eleven Bailey Bridges were to be erected over the forthcoming weeks, with the largest at Canty's near Berwick upon Tweed.

Sunday 22 August

Railheads were established at Dunbar, St Boswells and Tweedmouth for the delivery of goods to all parts of Berwickshire, while a bus service operated between Berwick and Tweedmouth and Berwick to St Boswells, via Ayton. A bus also operated between Dunbar and Berwick. These bus services ran at the former train times and ticket holders were able to use their tickets for full services, as well as for the conveyance of parcels and other goods. All railway supplies for the repair to the main line were now in place at Tyneside where it was then transferred up to the yards at Tweedmouth for distribution to the worst affected areas.

Monday 23 August

Berwick Auction Mart Co.'s cattle and pig sale had been switched to Berwick from Duns. Likewise the Wednesday sale of sheep would now also be held at Berwick Mart.

An interesting find near the South Bells Fishery at Paxton, by Berwick fisherman Thomas Quarry, was that of a copper plaque attached to the side of a hut which had been washed down the Whiteadder. The plaque, of very heavy copper, was inscribed in white enamel:

This hut was placed here in memory of John Melrose by his wife in gratitude for many happy days spent on the River Tweed, 1936.

The Bailey Bridge at Canty's would serve the county for many years, much longer than originally intended. (Lawson Wood Collection)

It was later discovered that the plaque was from a salmon fishing hut which belonged to Capt. J.C. Collingwood of Cornhill House, who lost two huts on the day of the flood.

The majority of claims for loss and damage centred around those personal losses within the overspill area of the Tweed Basin. Fishing shiels, boats and equipment came at the top of the list. Reinstatement of the river bed and bankings took a lower priority.

Tuesday 24 August

The estimated damage to roads and bridges from the flood on 12 August was £215,000.

Complete new bridges were required at Coveyheugh, Sisterpath, Neuk, Blackburn Burn, Duns Mill, Pait's Hill and major works at Blanerne, Cumledge and Jubilee (Ayton) bridges.

Hundreds of bales of clothing arrived at Berwickshire High School in Duns for distribution to the needy families. Now, almost two weeks after the flood, there were only a handful of families in the outlying districts which had not yet received any aid.

Clothing had come from all over the country and also from the American Red Cross; the standard of clothing was very high and everyone was well satisfied with what they received. The Ministry of Food sent three cases of Tinned Meat and two cases of Dripping to be used by distress victims as a gift from the *Australian Tramway & Motor Omnibus Employees Association*. Members of the Duns W.R.I. manned the enquiry desk continually at the school and were praised by everyone for their vigilance.

Minutes of the Vacation Sub-Committee of the Lord Provost's Committee, Town Council of Edinburgh, 24 August 1948:

> *The Sub-Committee considered the question of a contribution being made by the Corporation to the National Flood Appeal Fund for the relief of distress caused by flooding in the area of the city and other areas.*
>
> *The Sub-Committee resolved that a contribution of £2,000 be made to the fund under the powers in Section 889 of the Local Government (Scotland) Act, 1947.*
> *Andrew H.A. Murray, Lord Provost*
> (Edinburgh City Council Archive Department)

Minutes of the Courts of Directors, British Linen Bank, 24 August 1948:

> *It was intimated that, following an approach by the Royal Bank of Scotland to the Bank of Scotland, the latter had suggested a joint contribution by the Scottish Banks to the Lord Provost of Edinburgh's National Flood Relief Fund. The Court agreed to subscribe £250 to the Fund, provided that a like contribution would be made by each of the Scottish Banks. The Secretary reported that severe damage by floodwater had*

been caused to the Cumledge Mills of Laidlaw's Blanket and Tweed Mills Limited, customers at Duns branch. It was agreed that an expression of the Court's sympathy be conveyed to these old customers, and that they be informed that the General Manager would be glad to discuss the position with them, if desired.
(Bank of Scotland)

Minutes of the Bank of Scotland Board, 24 August 1948;

Edinburgh Lord Provost's Flood Relief Fund
The Board agreed that the Bank should donate £250 towards the Fund, it being understood that the other Banks in Scotland would give a like amount.
(Bank of Scotland)

Whilst the National Disaster Fund was gaining momentum, so was the smaller fund, opened by the Rev. A.M. Douglas, minister of Duns Old Parish Church and the Provost of Duns, Mr A. Tait. The Cumledge Mill Distress Fund had money pouring in by every post and when it reached the sum of £3,077 by the previous Friday it was agreed that any further donations, unless specially marked for Cumledge Mill, would be sent to the National Distress Fund in Edinburgh. This was somewhat of a political move as all of the funds collected were for the Cumledge Mill Distress Fund which was soon to reach over £6,000 with still nothing sent on to the National Distress Fund. In today's prices this is equivalent to a staggering £120,000. Reverend Douglas was said to have been 'overwhelmed' by the response to his appeal and 'was deeply gratified for all donations, which had come from all over the country.' A fund administration committee has been set up to arrange the distribution of the fund to those at Cumledge Mills.

The Lord Provost of Edinburgh, accompanied by the Town Clerk, visited the Burgh Chambers in Duns to discuss arrangements for establishing a liaison between the local fund and the National Distress Fund (wanting to get a share for the larger fund). It was agreed that only fifty per cent of any claim would be presented upon application to the central administration committee through the appropriate local channels. This disbursement was noted in accounts as a 'grant', although it was not intended to be repaid.

The relief fund set up by the National Farmers' Union of Scotland would benefit every farmer affected by the flood waters, as many have been completely ruined. As well as direct financial help, it was believed that a system of loans will be instigated to help farmers build up their stock losses and meet the heavy expense of building up the fertility of the soil.

The trains were running once more and not only that, a new record was set by British Rail. The Royal Scot had already resumed its non-stop run between London King's Cross and Edinburgh Waverly that summer with a mileage of 392.7 miles. After the disruption on 12 August, all trains were routed along the 'Waverly' route which was to add an extra sixteen miles onto the journey. Not too much greater distance you may think, but there were difficulties in traversing this route with a very

The Bailey Bridge at Reston Mill was soon erected and traffic once more could approach the village from its spur of the A1 trunk road. (Bill Cormack)

steep climb at Falahill and then a long run of ninety miles south to the water troughs at Lucker. Fortunately the speed restrictions on much of the line were such that no appreciable extra use of coal or water was used on the run.

Driver Stevenson took the No.60029 *Woodcock* skilfully through the speed restrictions and over the various cross lines through the scenic central Borders. He forewent the usual stop at Galashiels for replenishing the tender with coal and nursed the locomotive into Lucker with just enough water. Driver Stevenson made history by being the first driver to succeed in running non-stop along this extended route of 408.6 miles. Whilst this emergency was ongoing for the rest of the summer, no fewer than eight trains northbound and nine trains southbound successfully made the non-stop run.

Wednesday 25 August

Three Bailey bridges were now erected in Berwickshire. These were at Millburn, Syphon Bridge on the Great North Road and at East Greenlaw. The approach roads had been newly surfaced with tarmacadam and temporary lights were installed. It was hoped that the bridges at Reston Mill and Campmoor would be open in the following week. Weight restrictions were imposed at each of these bridges.

The Bailey bridge over the Syphon was built by the Royal Engineers on Wednesday night between the hours of midnight and 7 a.m. the road works were completed by the County Roads working staff by 11 o'clock that same morning.

Thursday 26 August

Hearts Football Club arrived in Duns to play a select side to raise funds for the Flood Victims Distress Fund. More than £100 was raised when the Hearts won four goals to three against an inspired Berwickshire Select XI. The teams were:

Select – Reid (Duns); Johnstone (Coldstream) and Davidson (Duns); N. Duff (Chirnside); Galway (Duns) and Craik (Duns); Tocher (Coldstream); Burns (Duns); Horsburgh (Eyemouth); Blaikie (Duns) and T. Duff (Chirnside).

Hearts – Watters; Fordyce and Darling; Adie and Armstrong; Durkin; Bauld; Newman; Newman and Buchan. The referee was Mr T. Dalgliesh.

Two weeks after the disastrous flood and the danger of the embankment bursting now completely past, Eyemouth people had two serious grievances to make. Firstly, they were greatly annoyed with the seemingly hundreds of officials who had invaded the County and ordered them to prepare for a 'Great Disaster', should the embankment break, releasing thousands of gallons of water. Secondly, they were annoyed with the adverse publicity that the town received from every national newspaper in the country. Hotel keepers and boarding house proprietors were all of the opinion that the publicity had ruined the season. One 'mine host' said the publicity had 'put the fear of death into some intending visitors'; nearly 100 bookings had been cancelled so far.

As the *Berwickshire News* reported later: 'One Door Closes And Another Opens.' Within the space of twenty-four hours when almost all of the bookings were cancelled, the caterers found the flooding had not put the 'fear of death' into other people and the town was literally invaded by many sightseers and others who immediately took over the cancelled rooms. A well-known boarding house owner said her neighbours and other boarding house owners were all rather narrow-minded when told of their statement on adverse publicity.

> *Publicity is one of the best things out and by this flooding we have received free adverts in nearly all of the big newspapers. I bet that next season will be a bumper one.*

Acting Chief Magistrate of Eyemouth, Bailie James C. Collin, said, 'I feel the position at Eyemouth [about to be destroyed] has been somewhat over-dramatised.' However, it was pointed out to him that perhaps the Royal Engineers were more suitably qualified than the townsfolk to comment on how real the imminent danger actually was!

On a brighter side, for the *Berwickshire News*, this was the 'Story of the Century', reporters and staff were all called in (one even came on leave from the RAF) to increase the manpower and get the story into press. Orders for copies came from all over the country for the *Berwickshire News* reportage of the flooding. This greatly increased sales and record profits were recorded with the newspaper group.

Finally, the threat of the embankment bursting was removed, police officers were withdrawn, emergency services were scaled down, the Peelwalls to Prenderguest road was reopened. Life slowly returned to normal, but for some, it would never be the same again.

MINUTES of MEETING of CENTRAL COMMITTEE
of the NATIONAL APPEAL FUND of the
LORD PROVOST of the CITY OF EDINBURGH
for the relief of distress from Flooding

Edinburgh, 26 August, 1948.
The Lord Provost of Edinburgh in the chair

Present:	**Lord Lieutenant**	**Convener**
Midlothian	The Earl of Rosebery	Mr. Robert Burnside
East Lothian	The Marquis of Tweeddale	Sir Humphrey Broun Lindsay
Berwick	The Earl of Home	The Earl of Haddington
Northumberland		Alderman W. Smith

In Attendance:-

Sir Patrick Laird, Secretary, Department of Agriculture.
Mr. W. Birrell, Department of Health.
Mr. John M. Loughran, National Assistance Board.
Mr. J. Anderson, Scottish Home Department.

The Lord Provost informed the meeting that since the '19th inst', the date of the meeting at which the National Appeal had been launched, he made contacts in a number of areas in the region within which it was known that serious damage had resulted from the flooding, and that he had in fact visited a number of these areas and had the opportunity of making these contacts personally. It had been ascertained that in addition to the Committee set up in Duns to deal with the damage and distress, particularly at the Cumledge Mill area, arrangements had also been made by Berwickshire County Council for the set-up of a local Committee, the Secretary of which is Mr Allan Prudden, Manager, Bank of Scotland, Duns.

At Eyemouth, local arrangements were in existence and contacts were to be made with the Town Clerk.

At Haddington, the situation was also well in hand, and the Town Clerk there was the official correspondent through whom arrangements were to be made..

The Lord Provost also explained that he had a communication from the

Town Clerk of Peebles, to whom he had explained the present position regarding the National Appeal Fund, and the extent to which it is intended that assistance will be given from time to time for relief in areas in Scotland or the north of Northumberland.

From information supplied by representatives at the meeting, the position would accordingly now be that, in the following areas, local arrangements had been made for dealing with the situation. These arrangements were particularly for the adjusting requests for assistance of the appeal fund and receiving contributions. The Central Committee of the Appeal Fund were in a position to give in response to these appeals.

Area of Locality	Official Correspondent and Treasurer
Berwick County (other than Cumledge Mills Area)	Mr Allan Prudden, Manager, Bank of Scotland, Duns
Cumledge Mill Area	Rev. Andrew M. Douglas, The Manse, Duns.
Eyemouth Burgh	The Town Clerk, Eyemouth
Haddington Burgh	The Town Clerk, Haddington
Bonnyrigg & Lasswade Burgh	The Town Clerk, Bonnyrigg
Musselburgh Burgh	The Town Clerk, Musselburgh
Dalkeith Burgh	The Town Clerk, Dalkeith
Penicuik Burgh	The Town Clerk, Penicuik
Northumberland	The County Clerk, County of Northumberland, Newcastle upon Tyne.

The Lord Provost reminded the meeting that the objests for which his National Appeal had been launched were:

1.   The Provision of those extras beyond what would be provided by local or national assistance in order to enable the victims of the damage to resume their normal lives by the supply or renewal of home comforts and necessities.
2.   Beyond the first object, and funds permitting, the Appeal would provide such essentials as were required and were not provided from other national or local resources to enable people to resume their normal occupation – e.g. tools, implements and other items.

The meeting also agreed that, funds permitting, consideration should be given to appeals for assistance from the National Fund towards meeting severe and extensive loss sustained by small shopkeepers or occupiers of small holdings, where the circumstances indicated that but for such assistance these distressed persons would be unable to resume their normal activities.

The Lord Provost informed the meeting that the amount of the National

Fund as at this date is £22,000. It appeared to him vital that immediate assistance should be given from the fund when local executives have set out on some such basis as before mentioned the need for assistance from the National Fund.

The Committee accordingly agreed that it was desirable to publicise in some way the arrangements which the Central Committee had made for dealing with appeals for assistance from the Fund, and also for intimating the dates at which it was proposed to commence distribution of the Fund, and it might also be, for closing the appeal.

Furthermore, and having regard to the National character of the Appeal Fund, the Committee were agreed that it was necessary to publicise the fact that it existed to provide assistance in any area of Scotland or Northumberland which might stand in need.

The Committee agreed that the City Chamberlain, Edinburgh, as Treasurer of the National Appeal Fund be authorised to open and operate a Bank Account with the Bank of Scotland.

Arrangements were made for immediate distribution of funds available to meet the needs in those areas from which certain preliminary information had been received regarding the extent of flood damage.

(Berwick Burgh Council Archives)

Friday 27 August

The erection of the five Bailey bridges in East Lothian by Army Engineers was now well underway. Although one bridge was only started at 9.30 a.m. at Kingside, it was completed by 1 p.m., which was two hours ahead of schedule. Work on the Whittingehame Saw Mill bridge was scheduled to take place over the weekend ahead and a third at Spilmersford was set for the following Wednesday. Edinburgh Territorial Unit, 585 Field Squadron, R.E., were erecting the bridge at Lint Mill near East Linton. Engineers saw no problems with the work ahead and planned to have all five completed by the end of the following week. A first instalment of £8,500 was received at Haddington for the fund administered by Provost Fortune, from the Lord Provost of Edinburgh's National Fund. This was to give immediate help to those most suffering in the town. The Committee in charge of the fund classified the claims into three different categories:

Class A   Those least affected by damage
Class B   Those more seriously and extensively affected
Class C   Those cases in which there has been practically total loss.

Sums to be handed out would be in the following distinction: £20 for those in category A; £50 for those in category B and £100 for those in C. As the fund progressed, a total

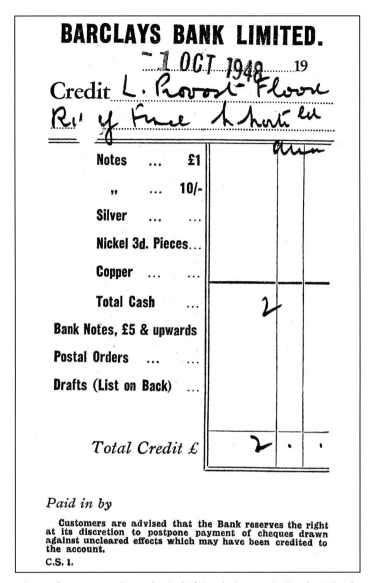

BARCLAYS BANK LIMITED.

1 OCT 1948 19

Credit L. Provost~Floor

Ru y Fuce Shorted

	Notes	...	£1
	,,	...	10/-
	Silver	...	...
	Nickel 3d. Pieces	...	
	Copper	...	...
	Total Cash	...	
Bank Notes, £5 & upwards			
Postal Orders	...	...	
Drafts (List on Back)	...		

Total Cash ... *2*

Total Credit £ *2* . ˙

Paid in by

Customers are advised that the Bank reserves the right at its discretion to postpone payment of cheques drawn against uncleared effects which may have been credited to the account.

C.S. 1.

Copy of a payment slip to the Relief Fund Account in Barclay's Bank, Berwick by the Burgh Council. (Berwick Burgh Council Archive Department)

of £16,796 15s was disbursed to householders. In addition to this, it was agreed that shopkeepers and smallholders should be treated separately within the account and a further £8,730 was disbursed to shopkeepers and £5,677 was paid out in agricultural losses. A further sum of £1,149 was paid to those who fell outside the categories, but were still treated as hardship claims. The Flood Committee in Haddington entertained over 400 claims for assistance, of which 250 were from householders.

NATIONAL ASSISTANCE ACT, 1948.

Certificate of Registration

𝔗𝔥𝔦𝔰 𝔦𝔰 𝔱𝔬 ℭ𝔢𝔯𝔱𝔦𝔣𝔶 that

....

being the Registration Authority under Section 37 of the National Assistance Act, 1948, have

registered.. ....

in respect of.. ....

situated at... ....

....

....
Clerk to the Local Authority

....19......

This Certificate shall be kept affixed in a conspicuous place in the Home.

W. H. & Co., Ltd., G.—N A 7.

A Copy of the National Assistance Board's application form for assistance. (Eyemouth Museum)

Copy of receipted payment made between the Berwickshire News *and Berwick Borough Council for their Flood Distress fund.* (Berwick Borough Council Archives)

Damage estimated done by the County Clerk at the time showed that over £10,000 of damage was sustained by private houses; £34,000 by local businesses and £4,000 to Burgh property. However, it would take another £100,000 to necessitate the repairs to roadways and bridges which were either damaged or totally lost that fateful day.

The first payments to flood victims under the Cumledge Mill Distress Fund was made, with the total fund at this time having reached £4,750. This money was intended to replace furnishings which may have been lost in the recent flood and another payment would be made at a later date to help provide personal belongings lost. The amount disbursed was £2,825. There were some grievances by householders whose property had been severely damaged. Payments were only available for household items and not for structural repairs as these should have been covered by personal insurance policies or by the company insurance policy under Cumledge Mill.

The access to the bridge at Abbey St Bathans was swept away and engineers were quick to check out how stable the rest of the structure was after the floods receded. (Margaret Squires Collection)

For all other cases, it was agreed that the National Assistance Board would carry out the inspection of all claims to the National Distress Fund. There was some dissatisfaction over a claim made by the Berwick Salmon Fishery Co. to the Lord Provost's National Distress Fund. Borough Councillors and other claimants were told that the direct appeal gained a disbursement of over £1,500 which included loss of wages and reconstruction of their section of the River Tweed. It was noted that all claims should have been made through the Borough Chambers and that any such disbursements should meet the agreed criteria for replacement of household and personal effects only. Other fishery claimants such as Ralph Holmes & Sons would receive no money towards river bank and river bed repair and further claims totalling £4,327 for river bed repair to the Tweed were also disallowed.

British Rail resources were now fully implemented and railway staff and engineers were supplemented by an additional three general contractors, plus the installation of accommodation for the now massive work force engaged in railway and bridge repairs. The target was now set for the full reopening of the line by 24 October.

Saturday and Sunday 28 & 29 August

Those people from Cumledge Mills who occupied the upstairs houses, returned home and it was hoped that the downstairs houses would be ready for occupation in a fortnight's time. During the following week, the floorboards were lifted and any flood water in the foundations pumped away. Berwickshire High School was finally closed on Saturday, having been used as an evacuation centre for all those affected at Cumledge Mill. Alternative accommodation, with friends and relatives, had now been found for everyone still not able to return home. Only two families were without friends to live with, but the County Welfare Officer Mr J.B. Arnott has found temporary accommodation for them in the district.

One of the greatest problems that occurred when a bridge was lost, was the consequent loss of electric and water supplies; these were a first priority before bridge repairs were initiated. (Margaret Squires Collection)

Monday 30 August

A team of sixty from the School of Military Engineering arrived to erect a Bailey bridge over the cracked and unusable Till Bridge at Doddington. Led by their Commanding Officer, Major Ford, they built and installed the bridge in just eleven hours. Paying tribute to the workers he said 'They are all administrative workers, most of whom have never helped to build a bridge before and some are even National Service Recruits.'

Tuesday 31 August

Members of the National Farmers-Union of Scotland recommended that they give assistance to the Flood Distress Fund, with priority to be given to those in dire distress, by providing personal goods and home comforts. Thereafter, depending on the support given, the fund would cover essentials – food, implements and other items to enable people to resume their occupation. The Union had been assured by the Department of Agriculture that everything possible was being done to facilitate a return to normal conditions in the flood damaged farming areas. The Union asked the Department for a special allocation of fencing, wire netting and cattle drinking troughs to be sold to farmers' suppliers in the south east.

To prevent the water spreading too quickly through the new sluice gates from the dammed water at Ayton, a sandbag wall 70yds long was installed to guide the flow of water. The clay banking was 52ft high and it was culvert No.146 which carried the Horn Burn tributary to the River Eye.

It was calculated that each foot of water would take twelve hours to drain, with the total release of the pent up water taking as much as three weeks. As this work progressed, the channel had to be deepened and its timber base and sides removed accordingly. 440 men were now officially employed in flood repair works, with many hundreds more volunteers.

Friday 3 September

An inspection of damage done to Eyemouth Harbour by the Development Commission Department's inspector revealed the following:

Sluice Gate Bridge – The tubular safety rails and stanchions were broken and carried away by trees borne down by the flood.
Centre Jetty – The tarmacadam surface of the roadway and the stone pitching underneath had been torn up and washed away along a length of 164ft. As a temporary measure, the deepest holes had been filled with quarry rubble to allow passage with care.

Even the tarmacadam road surface was ripped up along the length of the harbour quayside by the force of the water. (Margaret Squires Collection)

Fish Quay – The standards used for electric lights were all broken off and carried away by the flood waters and needed to be replaced urgently;

Inner Harbour Wall – This wall, which is a continuation shore-wards of the Fish Quay, was now in a much damaged and weakened condition from foundation to deck level of a length of about 450ft. The tarmacadam roadway and stonework was all washed away with the deepest holes now temporarily filled. Estimates by the consulting engineers were allowing £25,000 for the essential repairs and the Harbour Trustees were expected to make further application for increased grant money in light of this report.

Wednesday 8 September

Sappers from Ripon arrived at Canty's to start the construction of the Bailey bridge. A wooden roadway was laid down to the riverside to aid construction traffic and the pile-drivers would be in position in the next couple of days, after a small series of mishaps which delayed progress. The new bridge weighed 1,500 tons, was 440ft long and had five spans. Weight was restricted to forty tons and it was expected to remain in position for five years. Work was expected to start on the construction of the bridge, after all the supports were in place, on 27 September and the bridge would be open by 4 October.

Even the lampposts were knocked flat by the water's surge. Water pipes were also severed and it would be many weeks before the repairs were completed. (Margaret Squires Collection)

Monday 13 September

Following the damage done to the Duns Sewage Works by the flood, it was agreed to bring forward the scheme for the new sewage purification works at Duns. Covering the recommendations made by the Department of Health, Mr W. Renton, Town Clerk, said that costs would be in the region of £22,000. However, several local councillors expressed concern that the costs would be much greater than first quoted, going on past experience of other council works done.

Tuesday 14 September

President of the National Farmers' Union, Mr David Lowe, told members of how a Borders farmer told him his 'life work has gone', when he referred to the flood damage in the surrounding countryside. The case he gave was of a man who had ten acres, a small mill and 200 hens, a thriving little holding which had taken thirty years to bring up to its pre-flood state. He lost his hens and their houses, the land was destroyed completely and the mill ruined.

He was one of a small number of farmers who lost the very ground they grew their crops on. It was agreed that the General Purposes Committee of the NFU of Scotland should contribute the sum of £250 to the Lord Provost of Edinburgh's National Flood Relief Fund. The Chirnside Common Good Association raised £140 in aid of the Flood Distress, although it was uncertain at this stage who would benefit.

Wednesday 15 September

Following further heavy rain, the Rivers Whitadder and Blackadder rose sharply on the Wednesday afternoon and the wooden supports of the Langton Bridge on the Duns, Greenlaw Road, were swept away. The bridge was now closed to vehicular traffic, but pedestrians were still able to cross.

Berwickshire Police issued the following list of roads still closed: Duns – Preston, pedestrians only; Elmford – Cranshaws, closed; Swinton – Paxton, closed at Nabdean; Chirnside – Coldstream, closed at Milne Graden; Carfrae Road closed; Coveyheaugh Bridge closed; Edrom Road closed at Blanerene Bridge and the Earlston – Kelso road closed at Purves Haugh.

At one time the alarm was raised for the residents at Cumledge Mills. Householders said that they were prepared to evacuate once more if the raining continued all day. Fortunately the rain stopped at midday and the river level stayed just below the level of the bank. Special precautions had to be taken at Canty's Bridge to secure a pontoon raft carrying a pile driver being used for the temporary erection of the triple Bailey Bridge. Troops had to attach extra lashings to keep it steady in the swift current created by the flood water.

Thankfully all of the water pumps were now installed at the 'lake', supplied by the Metropolitan Water Board, these pumps were able to shift five million gallons of water a day. Progress was hampered however by the additional rainfall which made for very difficult working conditions.

Tuesday 21 September

As a result of the flood damage to Eyemouth Harbour, Trustees asked that further repair works should be undertaken beyond the £5,900 in grants from the Development Fund. MP J.J. Robertson also received a tentative enquiry for an ambitious scheme for a new deep water harbour, likely to cost over £500,000 (it took almost fifty years for this scheme to go ahead – at considerably more cost).

Dredging works had been almost carried out to the extent of some 9,000 cubic yards of sand and silt removed when the flood hit. Fortunately the *Dragon* was still at her berth in the harbour and was able to assist the further clearing of the silt from the

flood. It was hoped that a new 'sluicing scheme' would help to keep the harbour clear in the future, to allow developing flood water to assist in a natural clearing of the sand bank which collected at the harbour entrance.

Monday 4 October

Divers from Universal Divers Ltd of Manchester were called in to examine the foundations of Berwick Bridge and the Royal Tweed Bridge. At a cost of thirty guineas, excluding travelling expenses, divers worked in appalling conditions to check the undermined foundations and remove the log jam before the bridges were deemed to be safe and open to all traffic by foot, road or rail.

Opposite, above and overleaf: *Good progress was made to start the temporary and permanent rail bridges. Here work is progressing at Renton Smithy Bridge No.124 near Grantshouse.* (Margaret Squires Collection)

Good progress was made to start the temporary and permanent rail bridges. Here work is progressing at Renton Smithy Bridge No.124 near Grantshouse. (Margaret Squires Collection)

Tuesday 5 October

The Railway Executive announced good progress on the repair of many of the damaged bridges. Whilst work was progressing, long-distance trains were being re-routed through Kelso and St Boswells, adding another sixty to ninety minutes per train journey. Railway engineers, contractors and military bridging experts have been carrying out combined operations on a number of different rail sections. The water impounded by the railway bank between Ayton and Reston was continuing to be released through a specially cut trench. Aided by the Metropolitan Water Board pumps and equipment with technical assistance at the disposal of British Railways, the level of the lake was rapidly dropping.

Between Reston and Grantshouse, clearance was proceeding steadily and pile-driving was in hand at six of the seven bridges which were washed away. It would be April 1950 before the new permanent bridge would be opened in Grantshouse.

On the Eyemouth branch line, the land slips were soon cleared and work commenced on rebuilding the central support pier. This was constructed by driving steel piling 25ft into the rock and gravel to provide a permanent cofferdam in which the mass concrete foundation was laid 12ft below the level of the river bed. The new pier was built of a core of reinforced concrete faced in red brick. The other piers were also enclosed in new steel sheet piling. To further protect and enhance the existing piers, in light of the possibility of future flood damage, the river course was altered, Eyemouth Mill Laid had to be re-formed and a new cutwater was constructed as well as a new concrete wall carried down to bedrock along the river side of Pier No.5 and round one end as a further protective measure.

It took over ten months to complete the work and on 29 June 1949, Mr T.F. Cameron, Chief Regional Officer, Scottish Region, received Provost J.S. Collin of Eyemouth at the station. The 12.42 p.m. train was signalled out of Eyemouth Station by the Provost, after he had been introduced to the crew. The single coach was hauled by ex-N.E.R. 0-6-0 engine No.65039.

Interestingly, there were many hundreds of itinerant workers stationed in the Borders, many of whom appeared in the local courts for various breaches of the peace and drunk and disorderly conduct. Inspector Cruikshank prosecuting said,

> *This type of offence is becoming prevalent in Berwick. These men are employed on flood repair work and they are coming into town with money to burn. They then get drunken and quarrelsome and when advised by the police, in a friendly way, to go home quietly they become abusive'.* PC Steele corroborated this and said, *'I have never heard such language in a long time!'*

In front of two lady Magistrates, the guilty were fined £2 each.

Under the Department of Agriculture's chief of engineering Mr A.G. Ingham, *Operation Noah* had already begun to restore the flooded and damaged farmland. Excavators and bulldozers were assembled along the broken banks of the River Eye, ready to put the river back into its bed. Although restoration of the Eye's course was only part of the task, it was considered the most urgent and the authorities were concentrating on it first. Parts of Gala Water would receive attention later.

The situation was still considered so delicate that if only half the rainfall were to fall again at this time of the repair operations, the damage likely to be caused would be as great as the flood in August.

The State shouldered the financial burden on the land restoration scheme and this cost was likely to be in excess of £100,000. Replacement of lost farm stock was not included in this estimate, as it is not an accepted liability of the State. Farmers were be offered loans at 2½ per cent interest over three years to replace lost pedigree stock.

Several hundred acres were involved in the Eye area. In places, great piles of debris and boulders, some weighing between three and four tons, had to be removed. The most damaged area was the seven miles from Ayton to Grantshouse, where the work of realigning the river, clearing the debris and replacing fences and farm roads was already well underway. The cost of any improvements on the reinstatement work was negotiated with the landowners concerned. During a press conference at St Andrews House in Edinburgh, presided over by Sir Patrick Laird, it was reported that 165 improvement schemes had been approved under the Hill Farming Act, 1946 at a cost of £825,000.

The State offered a half share of the cost of the improvement schemes, but only on properties which were deemed as 'hill land'. 'Live' schemes – those approved or still to be considered – involved 1,003 farms covering 1,800,000 acres and works estimated to cost £1,776,000, with dilapidated roads and farm building bearing the brunt of the expense.

Saturday 23 October

As promised, the main line railway opened for traffic in both directions. The aptly named, Mr J.C.L. Train (later to become Sir J. Landale Train), member of the Railway Committee in charge of civil engineering, gave this confident report:

> *It can now be reported with confidence that the route between Berwick-on-Tweed and Dunbar will be available for goods traffic, as programmed, as from daybreak on Monday, October 25th.*

Construction work at bridges 137 & 138. (National Railway Museum, York. NRM 14/02 No. 126/26/64)

Work progressed rapidly: here the underway of reinforced concrete is being craned into position.
(National Railway Museum, York. NRM 18/02 No. 126/38/64)

It took only eleven weeks to make repairs, clear the lines, build bridges, alter the routes of rivers and get the trains running once more. For those who took part in this massive task, it still ranks as probably one of the greatest civil engineering achievements in the railway's history.

The Railway Magazine *Jan/Feb 1949*

> *The main line from Berwick to Edinburgh, which was severely damaged by floods in the second week of August was reopened for freight traffic on October 25, and for passengers on November 1. The passage of 39 daily freight trains during the first week helped to consolidate the track before passenger services were resumed.*

From 1 November most of the speed restrictions were eased from 15mph to 30mph and all passenger trains resumed running via Berwick and Dunbar, with savings in journey time of up to forty-five minutes. In view of the prevailing abnormal conditions, the reopening of the railway within eleven weeks of the disaster was a noteworthy achievement.

Above: Bridge No. 126 after the complete rebuild. (National Railway Museum, York. NRM 11/02 No. 126/21/64)

Below: At Harelawside, temporary bridge No. 125, LNER 61992 pulling heavy freight crossed the now quiet and subdued little River Eye. (National Railway Museum, York)

This engine with goods wagons was the first train to test the line and help consolidate the track. Here it passes over bridges 137 & 138 at Coveyheugh, to the north of Reston.
(Margaret Squires Collection)

Sir Eustace Missenden, Chairman of the Railway Executive, stated that the work already carried out between Berwick and Dunbar, and on branch lines, had cost about £300,000, and that permanent restorations of bridges probably would cost £400,000 more. Permanent bridges would not be ready for traffic next summer, and speed restrictions would still be in operation.

One of the biggest tasks in restoring the main line was the replacement, by temporary structures, of the seven bridges over the Eye Water, which pursues a meandering course, beside the railway, for about five miles between Grantshouse and Reston. The old bridges had an average span of about 30ft.

Five were of the masonry arch type, but two were wrought iron girder structures. Not only were the bridges demolished, but long sections of the adjoining embankments were washed away, leaving gaps of 120ft to 150ft across the river. The temporary structures therefore had to be much longer than the original bridges and have several

The 60012 passenger train seen here crossing bridge No.124 behind the 62706 to help consolidate the track before regular service could be resumed.

Testing the bridges at Coveyheugh. The logistics involved in completing the bridge works in such a short space of time was an engineering triumph for British Rail.

spans. Thousands of tons of filling were required to make good the damage caused by the series of landslides, slips and washouts between Cockburnspath and Grantshouse. Much of this material was taken from the land adjoining the railway by draglines and bulldozers. The land slips at Burnmouth were also receiving immediate attention.

To further reinforce the track at Burnmouth, another 8ft was cut into the hillside banking and a solid concrete wall was constructed to a solid rock foundation 27ft below ground level. Concrete blocks and steel sheet piles further secured the line and a new track was laid to carry the up line.

Quantitative studies undertaken a year after the deluge raised some important factors regarding the flood and its effects, some of which could possibly have been avoided. However foresight is a wonderful attribute, considering that those dealing with the enquiry had only the after effects to examine and year old memories! Surprising factors did come to light including the following:

The Whiteadder Water destroyed bridges within only two miles of its source.

The bridges across the Blackadder were destroyed because they were built at natural or artificial constrictions which impeded the escape of the flood waters.

North flowing rivers and tributaries formed erosion basins, whereas southern flowing rivers formed deposition zones, covering haughs with thousands of tons of gravel.

The angle of the land leading to the river sides contributed to the run off, particularly where the first bridge at Pait's Hill on the Eye fell under a volume of water it wasn't designed for.

Over 200 cases of road damage were reported.

Most slopes and gradients over 1:3 were unable to hold the water and all formed landslips to some degree.

Most farmers regarded the soil loss as negligible, but the water stained red from the Old Red Sandstone soils spread over two miles out to sea and it would be a number of years before the real effects of the flood were felt with the subsequent reduction in soil productivity.

Recent hill drainage schemes actually aided the flood rather than help avert it and the herringbone natural drainage of the Border hills undoubtedly speeded up the effects of the flood.

Had the surrounding hills been left to natural and planted forestation, the effects would have only been slight in holding back water, but over the large area affected, the results of this would have been considerable, but it is only a guess at what could have been averted.

The amount of work undertaken by the railway board was astronomical with over 6,500 tons of debris removed from the track and then reused to repair the river bankings. A further 50,000 cubic yards of filling was lain to restore subsidences, 2,000ft of new drains were lain, 1,750yds of sheet piling were driven into the ground,

Here the Flying Scotsman passes over temporary bridge No.125 at Harelawside, between Reston and Grantshouse on 1 November, headed by The Tetrarch, 'A3' class 4-6-2 locomotive No.60060. (Credit: National Railway Museum, York)

3,000 cubic yards of concrete were used in bridge repairs and 2,393 tons of steel were used for temporary works.

By the time the flood had subsided, more accurate estimations of agricultural losses were reached. Unfortunately, the loss of agricultural land and crops only doubled the agony of the local farmers, as they were hit by one of the most severe winter snow storms of the century. There was no fodder available for the livestock and in most cases no barns or sheds to house the stock, as most had not been able to be replaced.

The National Farmers' Union stated that there was a loss of 1,370,000 sheep; 30,000 cattle and 100,000 acres of wheat with financial losses of over £20,000,000. Upwards of 100,000 tons of potatoes were lost to the flood and it was a 'race against time' to plant and harvest crops before a similar disaster would befall the farmers the following winter.

Whilst these costs were being bandied about, the real cost of the trauma and the effect on the Borderers' lives would live with them for many years. Small farms would be bankrupt, boats sunk, houses swept away, businesses closed and many hundreds of jobs lost. What started off as a summer shower turned out to be the worst flood in over 100 years.

Report From Meteorological Office, Edinburgh: August 1948

At 06.00 on 12 August a shallow depression was centred off the Norfolk coast. This feature had moved slowly east-north-eastwards from its position just off south-west Ireland on the afternoon of 10 August. By 18.00 GMT on the 12th, the depression was centred in the North Sea. The exceptional rainfall was due to a combination of favourable circumstances resulting from the development north-westwards from the centre of the depression of a slow moving trough of low pressure. This trough extended to a considerable height, probably to around 34,000ft and was accompanied by a strong low level convergence and ascent of moist air which had become unstable because of the overrunning of cold air at higher levels. The resulting instability added further to the rainfall intensity, as did the orographic uplift of the strong north-easterly airflow by the high ground. The exceptionally heavy rain caused unprecedented flooding in the Border region of southern Scotland. Berwickshire and East Lothian were particularly badly hit. The Rivers Whiteadder and Tweed rose 16-17ft above normal. Near Kelso the Tweed rose 6 ½ inches above the highest previous flood mark which was recorded in February 1831.

The rainfall in the area during the period 6 to 12 August amounted to some 30% to 35% of the average annual amount at some locations. The heaviest twenty-four-hour fall occurred between 09.00 GMT on the 12th and 09.00 on the 13th; amounts measured at some places corresponding to around 20% of the annual average. Heavy rain also fell in the Tweed Valley on 7 August and thereafter the ground remained saturated because of poor drying conditions. This contributed significantly to the flooding resulting from the heavy rain during the 12th. (Meteorological Office, Edinburgh)

THE FLOOD

By kind permission of Wm Johnston, Buckie House, Cornhill. August 1948

We have read of floods and their after effect;
In years to come we'll treat floods with respect;
We've witnessed a sight we could not well credit;
The rain it came down as though it were leaded.
Each little brook became a great torrent;
With a splash and a dash, took all before it;
Every hillside became a great water shed,
As it tore great boulders and logs from their bed.
The rivers, well language fails to describe,
Old landmarks and bearings were left in their stride;
Houses that for years stood many a test,
Were carried away on the height of the crest.
Men awoke to find their chambers awash,
Whole families were forced to vacate with a dash,
Oil cloth and carpets were more or less ruined,
And themselves in danger of being marooned.
All Borders rivers were sights to behold;
They burst their banks and left a havoc untold.
Sheep from their grazings and cattle as well,
Just swept off their feet in this terrible swell.
Acres of corn, just ready to harvest,
Were covered by water and mud spoiled the rest.
Potatoes and turnips uprooted and spoiled
And grazings at least for a time being soiled.

Bridges have from their foundations been torn;
Circuitous routes to take with patience been borne.
Trains have also been forced to make a detour,
Improvised by bus to convenience the tour.
The last but not least is the scene on the beach
From round Spittal Point to the end of sight's reach.
Everything that one can think of has landed;
The dead and broken, most nameless, some branded.
In spite of terrible trouble and shock,
Men hasten again the wheel for to spoke,
Start once again the broken threads for to weave.
It makes things worse to sit down and to grieve.

Further Reading

The Berwickshire Coast: Lawson Wood, Stenlake Publishing
Eyemouth in Old Picture Postcards Volume I: Lawson Wood, European Library
Eyemouth in Old Picture Postcards Volume II: Lawson Wood, European Library
The Eight Minute Link: Lawson Wood, Ocean Eye Publishing

About the Author

Lawson Wood is local to Eyemouth and Duns in Berwickshire. He was born in Duns, brought up in Eyemouth and has lived and run businesses in both towns extensively. He is the founder of Scotland's first Marine Nature Reserve and a Fellow of the Royal Geographical Society. A Fellow of the Royal Photographic Society and Fellow of the British Institute of Professional Photographers, he is an internationally acclaimed underwater photographer and author of twenty-six books world wide for publishers such as New Holland, Reader's Digest and Lonely Planet. This is his second book for Tempus Publishing, the first being the highly successful *The Bull and the Barriers – The Wrecks of Scapa Flow*. Lawson is also the author of several other local history books detailing a photographic record of eastern Berwickshire.

Other Tempus Titles Include

The Bull & the Barriers – the Wrecks of Scapa Flow	Lawson Wood
Shipwrecks of the North East Coast Volume 1: 1740-1917	Ron Young
Shipwrecks of the North East Coast Volume 2: 1918-2000	Ron Young
Shipwrecks of the East Coast Volume 1: 1766-1917	Ron Young
Scotland's Malt Whisky Distilleries	John Hughes
Moon Over Malaya: A tale of Argylls and Marines	Audrey Holmes McCormick & Jonathan Moffat
The Royal Corps of Signals	Laurette Burton
The Black Watch	Blackwatch Regimental Museum
The Scots Guards	William F. Hendrie
Shipping on the River Forth	William F. Hendrie
Grangemouth	William F. Hendrie
Dunfermline	George Beattie
Rosneath & The Gareloch: Then & Now	Keith Hall
Around Doune and Deanston	Karen Ross
St Kilda – A Journey to the End of the World	Campbell McCutcheon

Following the examination, railway workers were called in to remove those rails and sleepers which hadn't already been lost to make way for the sappers to try and blow a hole in the embankment to reduce the water pressure on the other side. The top layer of the embankment was also taken up to remove some of the weight of earth bearing on the collapsed culvert.
(Margaret Squires Collection)